People a

GET FREE ACCESS TO OUR ONLINE BRANDING TOOL

READ THIS FIRST

Just to say thanks for buying this book, I would like to give you free access to my online tool that helps you monitor your online image.

TO ACCESS OUR FREE TOOL GO TO:

FootprintFridayTool.com

This tool will show you all the online results other people will discover about you.

Light, Bright

& Polite

FOR PROFESSIONALS

How to be your authentic self on social media
while making your employer proud

by Josh Ochs

Table of Contents

Chapter 1: How social media can hurt your career

"Everywhere I go, I'm second to arrive. My reputation precedes me, and sometimes it skips out on the bill." —Jarod Kintz

---

Here are some key takeaways from this chapter:

- **Often people underestimate their involvement with social media.** Everything you do online lives on in the public sphere, from your LinkedIn bio to your comments on friends' Facebook posts.

- **Most prospective employers—as well as current ones—can and will search for you online** to learn more about the person behind the resume (and make sure the person online and matches up with their resume). You want your online posts to show you're someone the company will be proud to associate with.

- **Assume that everything you share online could eventually be discovered** by your colleagues, clients, and employer.

- **People don't always tell you if something you post offends them** or raises eyebrows—but they will remember it.

- **Avoiding social media is not the answer.** People like to associate with other people who are engaged in their communities and can be "discovered" online doing positive things and showing their gratitude.

Maybe you just read that chapter heading, How Social Media Can Hurt Your Career, and thought, "This book is not for me. I am not very active on social media; what I do post is pretty innocent, and no one but my close friends and family members read my posts anyway."

If that sounds familiar, then guess what? This book is precisely for you.

Everyone has an online footprint (basically, what shows up when people search for you online), and what's contained in your footprint can shape your reputation—and hence your career—in ways you never anticipated.

Your footprint includes but is not limited to:

1. **Every social media profile you've ever created.**
   Facebook, LinkedIn, Twitter and Instagram are among the most commonly used by professionals, but there are plenty more

2. **Every comment or picture you've posted** or been mentioned in every comment or picture you've shared

3. **Online discussions you've participated in** / online groups you've joined

4. **Posts from other people** who have a similar name to yours

That's far from a comprehensive list of what goes into your online reputation, but it should cause you to pause and consider for a moment how much you've actually shared about yourself online without really thinking about the long-term repercussions.

Here's the thing: Social media is deceptively simple by design. We open our Facebook, Instagram, Twitter, Snapchat and other social media accounts, scroll through our friends' party pics, their funny stories about their day, and their comments on current events. Most of us like to be part of the conversation, and it's so tempting and easy to chime in with the first thing that pops into our head about our own experiences/observations/amusing anecdotes (that might not seem so amusing to others).

What could possibly go wrong?

Plenty. That's what this book is all about. I want to show you why social media is a wonderful and powerful tool—and like all powerful tools, it really ought to come with an instruction book complete with those warnings that often seem laughable ("Who would ever do that?"). The reality is that people post things on social media every single day that might seem like a great idea at the time but later turn out to have negative consequences in ways you never expected.

How your social media posts can get you kicked out of two countries

An acquaintance of a friend shared this story with me for this book. Here's a story about Lisa Coghlan:

I was born in Ireland and I moved to Australia for two years on a working holiday visa. I returned to Ireland for one year to figure out what I wanted to do for my career. I then applied for a 6-month holiday visa back to Australia to live with friends till I figured out what I wanted to do. Keep in mind, this wasn't a work visa, just a holiday visa.

After traveling for 24 hours from Ireland to Australia I was pretty tired. As I was going through immigration the Australian airport officials suddenly stopped me and asked me for more details. They wanted to know why I was visiting, why I didn't have return flights and what I was going to do while I was here on a non-work holiday. I proceeded to explain that I might go to New Zealand during the 6 months I was there. After giving them all my visa paperwork the officials called me over to a computer with a web browser set to Facebook.com on the screen. The woman told me to put in my details. I was thinking "there's no way they can snoop through all my private messages" but of course they did and straight away there was a conversation between myself and a friend. She was asking what my plans were in Australia and I explained "I'm not sure I just need a break but I might try to find a job."

Straight away the immigration officials highlighted this. The officials had already confiscated my phone and they proceeded to look up the name of the person meeting me at the airport and told her to go home since I wouldn't be leaving anytime soon. I wasn't aware this was happening.

I was brought into a room and interviewed for about four hours waiting to hear their decision. They proceeded to decide to cancel my visa and slap me with a three-year ban! I am not allowed to visit Australia for 3 years!

Then they gave me a bright orange jacket and escorted me out the back entrance of the airport into a bus and brought me to a detention center where I had to remain until they could contact my airline to organize my flight home.

When I arrived they searched my bags and all I was allowed to keep was pj's and underwear and was given a card with $20 on it to spend in the detention 'shop.'

I spent two nights in the detention center which had 4 Irish lads each with their own crazy stories. The next morning I awoke to an English girl in my "cell" sitting next to me who looked at me and said, "You also in here because of Facebook?"

There were also some crazy people in there for stabbings and other assaults. We were put in the same cell.

My best bet was to fly to China. So off I went to Guangzhou International Airport and after landing, I quickly realized they weren't allowing me to exit the plane. They gave me no explanation, but after 1.5 hours they allowed me to deplane and then they told me I wasn't welcome there. China heard that Australia didn't want me and they were basically kicking me out without even letting me visit. I told them I'm going to Bali so we verbally agreed I cannot return to China (I still have no idea what actually happened there but after 11 hours in that airport it was not fun). They kept my passport and luggage up to one hour before I boarded the flight from China to Bali.

Tactical Tip: Everything you put online (even in private messages) can eventually be discovered and become public. In this rare case, Lisa's travel plans were completely changed by simply mentioning that she might consider getting a side job (when her holiday visa expressly prohibited such an action).

One of the most common mistakes is to imagine that when you post on your social media accounts, write in your blog, comment on a message board or do anything else that becomes part of your online footprint, you've somehow entered a different realm—one that can be kept separate from your professional or "official" life. Maybe you seriously doubt your supervisor, colleagues, clients or potential future employers (much less immigration officials) would ever bother looking at what you do online in your "private" space. Maybe you even believe that if they do look and find something you've posted that they don't particularly like, they'll somehow keep it separate from the way they view you as a professional. In a perfect world, maybe they would. In the real world, it's very difficult for people to forget unsettling things they've discovered about somebody's personal life, plans, activities or attitudes, no matter how they come across it. (And before you get indignant about that, consider this: It's not as if employers break into employees' homes and snoop through their things. They're just looking at information that you've made freely available on the Internet.)

Let's start by dispelling a few common myths about social media and how it could impact your career.

Myth #1 - Employers have access to my resume, education, experience, and talent—not what I do in my free time.

Unfortunately, this is wrong. Studies have shown that the majority of hiring managers look at (and are easily able to find) a candidate's online social profiles as part of the evaluation process. And they have good reasons for doing so. Every company has made a poor hiring decision at some point and paid a price for it, including hiring employees who have damaged their reputation, employees who have hurt company morale, and more. So no matter how well you come across on your resume and in an interview, it only makes sense they want to know more about the person behind the resume. Do you freely express political views that might offend some clients or colleagues? Are you intolerant of people who are different from you? Do you seem to spend a great amount of your free time in bars, or wearing risqué clothing? It might seem like an invasion of privacy, but it's hard to fault employers for using information that's easily enough accessed online to protect themselves against potential problem hires. In other words, employers do want team members who are authentic and have well-thought-out opinions to share in appropriate ways and situations, but they don't want employees who always seem to be on the edge of alienating others or distracting from a professional, productive workplace.

By the way, if you already have a great job, all the reasons for holding your online activities to the standard I call Light, Bright, and Polite® (more on that later) still apply. If you're looking for a promotion—within your company or somewhere else—your employer will very likely check again. After all, if they're thinking of giving you more responsibility and a higher profile to go with it, your online reputation (professional and personal) is all the more important.

Myth #2 - My social media friends and I tend to have the same views on politics and other hot-button topics, so it's unlikely I'm going to offend anyone.

This might be a good time to ask how many friends you have on social media. For a lot of us, the number of friends we have on Facebook alone is well into the hundreds (and in my case, several thousand). Chances are pretty good that over time your Facebook friend list has come to include an awful lot of people you actually know very little about—including their views on politics, religion, Chinese food, Taylor Swift, Kanye West or Beyoncé. I could go on, but you get the point. When you first signed up for Facebook, you probably went out of your way to build up the largest friend list possible. After a while, adding new friends or accepting friend requests from others just became habit (especially as Facebook encourages you to do so). There's nothing wrong with that—but you can no longer claim to know your audience when you casually post a rant about something that annoys you, reveal overly personal details about your life or say just about anything that could be seen in a negative light.

Meanwhile, no matter how gratifying it is to see when your friends "like" and offer positive feedback on your posts, you can't assume that represents anywhere near a full picture of what your audience thinks as a whole. Many of your friends and acquaintances are too shy to disagree publicly on your posts. In fact, many may be silently disagreeing with you but don't know how to show it without calling unwanted attention to their own views or even starting an argument. In other words, many of your online friends may realize that their social media is not a place to post these rants.

Myth #3 - My boss/potential boss and I aren't friends on Facebook, so she has no access to what I post (and no right to see it).

This is false on many levels. Facebook and other forms of social media change their privacy rules frequently, so chances are that at any given time, you're probably not entirely sure what's private and what's public anyway. Also, Facebook and other social networks are rewarded by search engines when they share more of their users' content publicly so people can find it on the web. Facebook secretly wants your info to be discoverable by the biggest search engines so people can visit your page (and advertiser viewership can increase).

But let's assume that in theory what you just posted on social media is not going to show up in your employer's news feed.

So far, so good. But what about the friends you have in common? If you work at the same company, chances are enormous that you at least share friends on Facebook—and if one of those contacts shares your post, or if you post on one of their comments, that will show up in your boss's feed (this happens every day). And it's not just your boss you need to be thinking about—it's your clients, colleagues, or any professional contacts with whom you want to be on good terms (and who communicate with your boss). So if one of your friends goes off on a political rant that's offensive to people with different political leanings, and you comment on it (or even just "like" it), you've just inadvertently brought your political views into the office and possibly alienated people whose professional support you value.

Political posts, again, are among the worst offenders, especially at a time when politics are as polarizing as ever. But think further down the list of topics that initially seem innocent enough but can still offend somebody, somewhere. Think about it a moment—or even take a second and check your Facebook or Twitter feed right now—and it probably won't take you long to come up with examples of comments or photos you've seen others post—or maybe posted yourself—that have the potential to offend if seen by the wrong eyes.

How to get fired with one tweet

Cisco Job Opportunity

I'll give you possibly the most famous example of the "my boss (or potential boss) will never see this" myth, and how someone lost an opportunity by believing she had control over where her tweets landed. A young woman graduated from a good college and found that Cisco was interviewing. She applied online, got asked to come in for an interview, and they made her an offer. What do you think she did next? She went to Twitter to publicly express both her excitement and concerns: "Cisco just offered me a job! Now I have to weigh the utility of a fatty paycheck against the daily commute to San Jose and hating the work," she wrote.

Now, just for a second, think about how many other candidates they must have said "no" to in order to say yes to this young woman. Perhaps 20-100 candidates. I ask students in my speeches, "Do you think it's generous when a company says "no" to all of those other people and says "yes" to you?" They all nod their heads in unison.

"Do you think it makes the company feel good to see a tweet like this?" Probably not.

Companies of all sizes are trained to pay attention online to see if one of their customers is mentioning their product or service in a way that they need to address.

In this case, one of the senior level employees noticed the

tweet and responded with: "Who's the hiring manager? I'm sure they would love to know you will hate the work. We are versed in the web."

Do you think she got this job? No, she didn't.

You might be saying, "Josh, you're being way too hard on this young woman. You're using her as a bad example. You said she went to a good school and had a good resume. She could probably go anywhere to interview at another company."

Yes, you're probably right, she could interview anywhere. But do you think the next company she interviews at would search for her online?

Yes, they most likely will.

And here's what they will find... This one tweet has become the number one example to teach people how to get fired with just one post. It was picked up and written about in a negative way by CNN, ABC News, NBC News, Huffington Post, Time.com and many more outlets.

Now, when you search for this young woman's name, you see these news outlets clogging her Google results.

If you were to see these types of negative results when searching for someone, would you think they were full of positivity and gratitude? Probably not.

What she did sounds crazy, right? You would never do that, would you? Probably not. But pretend for a moment you received a job offer and you really were conflicted about it. Or maybe you let down your guard just enough to imagine that all the dangers you've heard about careless posts on the Internet are completely exaggerated, and that really and truly, only your best friends will see this. Social media is so much a part of our daily lives that for a lot of us posting our first reactions to things can feel like no more than a few lines scribbled in a diary. So yes, it is conceivable you could make a mistake like this in the middle of a perfect storm of a bad mood, bitter feelings, stress or whatever it is. Realizing that no one is immune to social media mistakes is an important reminder never to let your guard down online, especially in a sensitive, high-stakes matter like this.

Myth #4 - If I have a valid complaint about my company, it would be fake for me to hide it. I want to express my feelings online.

Ask yourself this: Do you have to air your public laundry in order to be honest? Given the number of hours most of us spend at work and the stress we might be experiencing, it's perfectly normal to have negative feelings from time to time about anything from company policies that you disagree with to the coworker who's really getting on your nerves. But even if you're disgruntled to the point of drafting a resignation letter, consider these possibilities:

(1) You might think better of the situation in the morning, and yet that raw, negative post will still be online—probably being passed around among your peers in the industry. Who can resist gossip like that?

(2) Potential new employers could rightfully doubt your discretion and loyalty. If you were willing to publicly trash your last employer, can they really trust you won't do the same to them? Employers believe that past behavior is a predictor of future performance.

Think about someone you admire, such as a well-respected company executive in your field. Can you imagine them sending a tweet publicly blaming their marketing team for a failed product roll-out? If they were in the habit of airing their concerns and complaints for all to see, they probably wouldn't be where they are today.

Myth #5 - But I would never post anything about my employer, so my online activities don't affect my career.

Don't be so sure. The pictures, information, sentiments and comments you share online can still affect your company regardless of whether or not the comment involves your company, your industry or anyone in it. Most companies place an extremely high value on maintaining a clean image, free of controversy. This helps that company attract more customers, and limits possible PR nightmares that could come out of social media blunders. If you jump into the fray on political or other hot-button topics on a social media site or message board, then by association you're interfering with your company's desire to stay free of controversy. No, you probably don't sign your posts Hermey, Toy Inspection Manager at Santa's Workshop. But if people don't already know where you work, they can easily find out by cross-referencing your name and profile across different networking sites like LinkedIn (or just Googling your name).

And if people decide they don't want to do business with your employer because of you, you've just become a liability.

The smaller the company, the bigger a problem it is—but on the other hand, the larger the company, the more people there are in HR who might eventually get wind of the controversy.

Notice that I didn't give a specific example of a post that might hurt your reputation within the company. The point is that it doesn't take much. If you're taking the time to read this book, I'm going to assume you're a thoughtful, conscientious person who wants to avoid offending others. But you can't be an expert in every cultural taboo or everyone's personal sensitivities. As an example, if you are tweeting during the holidays, there are a lot of opportunity for missteps. Tweeting warm sentiments about the Christmas season on the first day of Hanukkah, for instance—forgetting that several of your co-workers are Jewish—is an easy way to come across as tone deaf, even if it's completely unintentional.

That's why I always recommend—and your employer will appreciate—a healthy amount of caution when it comes to what you put out there for the world to see.

It's always wise to ask yourself: Is this Light, Bright, and Polite®? And always keep Murphy's Law in mind—if it could offend someone out there, assume it will. If it could be seen by your employer, assume it will. No matter how witty you are, or how many of your friends hold exactly the same political/social/other views as you do (as far as you know), social media is not the place to push your luck with controversial topics.

So if you want to express something that doesn't belong in the public sphere, instead consider calling or texting a friend instead of posting on a site where you have no control how far your words will travel.

Myth #6 - No one's complained about anything I've posted online, so I must be doing okay.

My response to this is, how do you know?

My primary purpose in this chapter has been to demonstrate how easy it is to offend others without meaning to. And here's the point: You won't always know. If a prospective employer decides against hiring you because you come across online as a person who lacks good judgment or discretion, they won't tell you. Their HR department knows their lawyer will advise them not to tell you they searched for you online and found negative posts/images. This would be a legal headache if you sued them. Instead, they simply say, "We found a better fit for our position; we will keep your resume on file." The same goes for being passed over for a promotion, not being included on a new task force and any number of other ways you might notice that your career isn't exactly taking off the way you'd hoped. Opportunities seem to pass you by. Posts that your employer, colleagues or clients find offensive—but never mention to you—are what I call Silent Opportunity Killers (SOKs), and while they might be silent, they're all too real.

Myth #7 - I'm not into social media at all, so none of this

really applies to me.

Ever heard the expression, "Sometimes silence speaks louder than words?" If you've read this far, you understand that employers, potential employers, colleagues, clients and others regularly go to the Internet to find out more about people beyond their resume, title or impressive education. By avoiding social media, you're not necessarily protecting yourself from scrutiny—you might be inviting more when they go to search for the "real you" and come up empty handed.

The first thing to understand is the difference between privacy and discretion. Some people avoid social media because they don't want to look like show-offs, or they want to protect their privacy. And it's absolutely true that you want to avoid posts that come across as self-centered, judgmental of others, shallow, or insensitive.

But what about all the opportunities the Internet presents to post pictures, comments, blogs and even videos that will reflect well on you, your character, your involvement in the community or your industry? These things make you attractive to employers who want someone who can bring that kind of positive attitude and community engagement to the workplace. If people search for you and find little or nothing, they're not going to assume you're a great person who's "secretly" out there trying to make the world a better place. They're just going to wonder why you appear antisocial.

If you are an introvert by nature—plenty of us are—the

Internet is actually a blessing in disguise. You can share your knowledge and interests with articles or helpful comments you add on different platforms, or show your community involvement with a group pic from a recent community project you helped with (putting the limelight on others rather than yourself). These are among the many ways you can use the Internet to show the good qualities and assets you can bring to a team while still being your authentic self. At the same time, you're giving potential employers something positive to discover rather than leaving them guessing.

Notice that I never suggest people avoid social media altogether—quite the opposite. There are a lot of ways you can have fun on social media in ways that help your career and be true to your authentic self. I'm going to show you how to have fun online while still impressing your company, professional peers, clients, and future employers—and even attracting new opportunities.

Are you monitoring your online image?

Register for our FREE Footprint Friday tool to manage your online brand each week in less than 5 minutes.

Visit FootprintFridayTool.com

Chapter 2: How to respond to negative posts

"Negativity spreads faster than any Justin Bieber song."
—Vanilla Ice

Here are some key takeaways from this chapter:

- **Search for yourself online regularly**, so you'll always know what others are going to find.

- **Make sure everything you post is full of gratitude and positivity.** Positive posts make a good "digital first impression" on people who could eventually impact your career.

- **You can't control others' actions, but you can always control how you react to anger and negativity.** Being polite under difficult circumstances always reflects well on you, online or off.

- **Being gracious and authentic online is usually a good indicator of how you handle situations in person.** It reflects well on your character and can lead to great career and personal opportunities.

Love it or hate it, social media is a powerful tool that has changed much of how the world works today. As we discussed in the last chapter, the choices you make online can have a tremendous impact on your future, either for good or for bad. The good news is that you're in the driver's seat when deciding what to post and how to frame it in a positive light. The better news is I can give you the inside information you need in order to use social media to boost—not damage— your professional reputation while still being your authentic self online.

I'm going to share with you the techniques I've learned from personal experience along with advice from influential industry leaders and words of wisdom from people who've learned the hard way what not to do when it comes to social media. As Eleanor Roosevelt once advised, "Learn from the mistakes of others. You can't live long enough to make them all yourself."

My campaign for public office

In May of 2009, I made a decision to run for Hermosa Beach City Council (a small beach community in Los Angeles). After living in Hermosa Beach for several years, I knew we needed to make changes to help businesses and residents in tough times. My decision to run was not an easy one. At the start, I was relatively unknown by community leaders. I was up against eight-year incumbents and candidates with experience in three past races. Essentially, all of them were well-known. I set out to knock on 3,015 doors and meet voters at their homes to try and make a name for myself.

Along the way, I got a call from a close friend asking "Did you see what someone wrote about you online?" I quickly went to

Google, searched for myself and couldn't find anything negative, so I called my friend back and asked how they found the info. I quickly learned that my friends (and perhaps local voters) saw a very different version of Google results than I did. In fact, they could easily find negative press about me on their first page of Google. I had to scroll through 5-6 pages to see the same negative results my friends were talking about.

I learned that I was searching for myself online using the wrong technique. Once I learned a better way, I was able to see what others were discovering when they searched for me online. **As a result, I learned how to curate and manage the first page of my Google results, which is the most important online resume a person has—far more important than a paper resume (or candidate brochure) that I may have spent hours crafting.**

As the youngest person on the ballot, I knew that I understood the Internet better than others. I also knew that when people would see my sign on a house or my brochure on their doorstep, they would want to learn more. They would think to themselves, "Josh seemed nice, but let's go find out who he really is by searching for him online and seeing what others say about him." My online search results were the next step to them forming their opinion of me and created a digital first impression, setting the stage for them deciding if they were going to vote for me.

I set out to make sure my online results were full of other people saying positive things about me. I made sure that everything I posted was full of gratitude and positivity. I also learned that it's important to curate your Google results long before you need them, so you can manage them before it really counts. I learned that I needed to search for myself online each week to see what I could find (and what others may see).

I also went back to the negative feedback that my friends had alerted me to—those posts that I wasn't seeing until I learned to improve my search techniques. They were coming from two Hermosa Beach residents who were blogging negative things about me. I realized they had never met me, and although I accepted I might never win their vote, I strongly believed they could at least respect my hard work and change their opinion when they learned that I had the community's best interest at heart.

I emailed them both and asked if they would meet me for coffee in the next few days to sit down and talk about the issues. Only one of them responded, and they said: "No, I'm not interested in meeting with you. I will ask you questions during the public debate next week."

Why would someone not want to meet with me but continue to write negative things about me online? I talked with my friends and campaign team and they all agreed we should move on and be positive. Needless to say, the bloggers' online comments and negative response still hurt my feelings.

At the debate, I sat on stage among the group of seven candidates. I was scared and nervous as residents came up to ask questions. Most were nice until one of the negative bloggers approached the mic to ask the group a question.

She said with a stern face, "I want to ask Josh Ochs a question." She proceeded to tell me how young I was, how I had no experience, and then threw in a question that was asked in such a scathing tone that it was clearly meant to throw me off guard.

I had every right to be offended and not care about her opinion. However, I responded to her question with a simple "Hello, how are you tonight?" I treated her like she was the only voter in the room and began show that I was genuinely interested in her question and her concern. I answered with poise, was kind and did my best to make sure she was pleased with my response. Unfortunately, nothing I said changed her opinion that night. By the look on her face, she was set on making me squirm on stage.

At the end of the debate, a nice woman came up to me and said: "Hi Josh, I wasn't going to vote for you yesterday, but now I am." I said, "Thank you. Why is that?"

She proceeded to tell me. "None of us like that woman who asked you the obnoxious question in the debate. In fact, we all know how she behaves and we don't agree with most of what she says. However, you were so gracious with her that we learned more about you than we could have otherwise. We learned that you are nice and courteous to those that are mean to you. You have my vote and the votes of many of my friends in the back of the room."

There's a key lesson I learned here: How you respond to people is more important than what they say to you. Voters were watching how I reacted to the blogger's outlandish remarks, and they were judging my response more than what she said. I quickly realized the more respectfully I treated the upset blogger, the more loyalty I was winning from other people. In fact, if the blogger wasn't mean to me, I perhaps wouldn't be able to show off how courteous I could be to everyone.

It was in that moment that I learned how powerful it is to be Light, Bright, and Polite® to others. The whole world would eventually see my actions, so I needed to make sure I was proud of what they'd see.

In some ways, this is easier said than done. We all have natural, human responses to other people speaking badly of us—especially when their words and actions are unjustified, and they appear unwilling to consider that there might be another side to the argument. But the reality is that some people really are unwilling to consider other people's opinions, and you could argue all day long without getting any closer to changing their minds.

Letting things go on social media

On social media, sometimes you have to make a conscious effort to ignore people who seem to be trying to get under your skin, whether they hurl direct criticisms at you (as my few but active detractors did during my city council run) or constantly post things that offend you. You might feel an obligation to stand up for your beliefs and for fair treatment, but social media is rarely the right context. If you feel the need to rant, call or text a friend. If you know the person who is making offensive comments and can reach out to them privately, it might be worth a try, but very little good will come from engaging in a social media war.

Here's why:

This may be a person (or people) with their own agenda or reason for lashing out, and it may be completely beyond your control.

When other people are negative, rude, dramatic, combative, etc. on social media, more often than not it reflects badly on them. Responding to them in like manner can also reflect badly on you—even if you're in the right. Remember how many people might be watching your mini-drama play out, and most will have no idea what it's about, who launched the first missile, or even care who has the better argument. All they'll see is that you're acting like someone who can't seem to rise above an argument that's probably not worth it and is rarely constructive.

If you let yourself get pulled into an argument, it gets harder and harder to get out of it. Others will respect you more for walking away from an online argument.

Employers—or anybody whose respect you want to earn—want employees who are drama free, and drama that another person tries to start will usually go away on its own if you let it.

As for my campaign, I ended up losing the election to the incumbent mayor by about 350 votes—but in the end, I gained much more from the experience than I lost. My reputation following the campaign was even more positive than when I started because of how I conducted myself, and how I was able to use social media to shine online even when I had obstacles to overcome. I quickly grew a following on my email list, Facebook, and every other network. As the underdog, many business owners and community leaders were rooting for me.

Several months after the election, I received invitations to help manage social media accounts for many businesses. One of the businesses was the very newspaper that reported on me during my council race. And now, I get the opportunity to travel the country to share how to shine online with 30,000+ students (and 5,000+ parents/professionals) every year. Our techniques have been adopted by over 3,500 businesses and approved by schools and colleges across the country. They have a vested interest in seeing their employees and students put their best foot forward online.

So while you might not be running for politics in the near future, in this book I'm going to show you how my digital footprint tips can be used to help you improve your career with positive online results.

Chapter 3: How to see your online results as others see them

Here are some key takeaways from this chapter:

- **Building relationships is important in most professions.** Social media is a great way to show that you are engaged with the community.

- **Make sure your LinkedIn account is current and accurate.** This should be an ongoing effort. A LinkedIn profile that's full of spiderwebs makes you look lazy and raises questions about what's accurate and what isn't in your resume. And if you don't update it regularly, you miss opportunities to ask for endorsements while successful projects are still fresh in the minds of (a) clients who were happy with your work, (b) representatives from nonprofit organizations where you helped make a positive difference, or (c) others who might be happy to share your positive contributions or attributes.

- **Find out the best way to search for yourself online** to get the most accurate picture of what others will see when they search for you. Also, ask a friend to look over your search results with you. They might see problem areas that you miss.

- **Improving your digital footprint should be an ongoing process.** You should always be aware of what shows up on the first two pages of your search results and work to make them as strong and positive as possible.

- **Always look for new opportunities to share group photos** from a recent volunteer effort or to post news about something positive your favorite (non-controversial) community organization has achieved, complete with gratitude for the opportunity to be involved in the event. New posts that show your positive, authentic self engaging with the community help keep your search results fresh and relevant.

While employers and clients may appreciate the impressive information contained in your resume—and the way you present yourself when you're in "professional mode"—they also know they'll get a more complete picture if they look beyond your resume and interview. To find out more about the "real" you, they're turning to the Internet. This is why you need to stay one step ahead by presenting yourself in the best possible light online, too.

How I do I know employers really take the time to check out job candidates' online profiles? I ask them.

I've made a career of learning how the decisions people make online affect their lives offline—beginning with my own experience as a political candidate. I also have seen how offline life choices can affect your online reputation. I constantly talk with online safety experts to find out how teenagers can stay safe online; I learn from college-admissions experts about how a teen's online reputation can help or hurt their college and even scholarship opportunities; I ask company founders how they work to maintain and improve their business' reputation with savvy use of social media.

Most importantly for purposes of this book, I talk whenever I can with employers about what they're looking for when they search for job applicants online.

How to shine online in the real estate industry

One of these employers is Chris Mygatt, president of Coldwell Banker Residential Brokerage Colorado.

Chris Mygatt oversees the daily operation of the state's largest real estate and relocation company, and he took the time to share his valuable insight into how the company uses online searches as a major factor when evaluating candidates:

"Each year we associate around 250 licensed real estate agents to our company. Although our prospective Realtors complete a thorough application, interview with a branch manager and ultimately complete a personality assessment, we are finding that a careful review of the candidates' social media sites offers us the most accurate picture of their true character. We've discovered that while it may be easy to create a compelling resume, many lack authenticity. It's almost impossible to hide your true character on social media. Much can be discovered about people on social media. The resume carries little more value than that of a paid advertisement in today's association process.

We focus our search and review of Realtor candidates on Facebook, Twitter, Instagram and LinkedIn. We also Google their names and look at what comes up on the first two search pages.

We understand that this is what current and future clients will be doing, and we want to know what they'll be finding out before we allow the Realtor to brand themselves with the Coldwell Banker name. With regard to Facebook, we first look to see if they have a page and a profile. We look at total friend count (or likes on a page), the number of posts in a given week and the types of things they post. Do the posts contain photos or video? Are they self-centered or outreaching?

Are they positive and inclusive? Do they have any engagement with people on their posts? We quickly review their photos ··· you'd be amazed what we find there. With Twitter, we are looking for regular engagement. Use of photos and video. Perception of expertise. With LinkedIn, is it current and accurate? Again, do they engage with people? With Instagram, is their account public or private?

When I'm looking at a prospective Realtor's social media accounts I want to see optimism. I look for what they are offering others. I don't want their posts to be egocentric, judgmental or polarizing—experts steer clear of politics and religion. It's important to be inviting on social media. We look for Realtors that "stay IN curiosity and OUT of judgment."

Independent Realtors are salespeople. To be successful they need to be engaging with a large network in a positive and supportive way. They need to be community leaders and knowledgeable, as well as interesting and interested in the industry. We can verify the authenticity of this in a matter of minutes with social media. If they have a limited presence on social media it makes them look like they haven't taken the time to build relationships to expand their book of business.

When we associate a real estate agent with our company, we are allowing that individual to leverage our brand and its 110-year legacy. We can't afford to take that lightly. A social media review gives us more confidence. With Realtor candidates, we are not necessarily looking for social media expertise, but we are looking for authenticity."

> Mygatt is using his own experience with evaluating Realtors, but his advice offers an inside look into what employers in all industries are doing today.

Be sure you caught the key takeaways:

1. "The candidates' social media sites offer us the most accurate picture of their true character." No matter how positive you appear in person, online postings that don't meet the Light, Bright, and Polite® standard will undermine that.

2. "We Google their names and look at what comes up on the first two pages." The good news is that employers aren't likely to spend all day looking for "dirt" on the fourth or fifth page of your Google results; they're usually satisfied with what they discover on the first or second. The bad news is that you have little control over what appears on the first or second page—Google does. That's why I'm going to show you in a minute what you can do better curate those first two pages, but you can take the first step now just by vowing going forward to present yourself online in the way you want potential employers to see you.

3. "If they have a limited presence on social media it makes them look like they haven't taken the time to build relationships to expand their book of business." I can't tell you how many people want to argue with me on this point—but now you have it straight from the source: Avoiding social media is not the best way to maintain a good reputation. As Chris stated, all that does is establish you as someone who doesn't understand the value of

building relationships and engaging with your community.

4. "Is their LinkedIn account current and accurate?" Good question. Considering that your LinkedIn account truly is your online resume, it's amazing how lazy people can be with it. Maybe you get a few points for having created a LinkedIn account, adding a decent photo and including your most impressive accomplishments. But do you solicit recommendations? Do you update it to include new information? Do you monitor it to make sure no one has added anything you don't want to be included? Does it mirror the resume you've just passed around the conference table during your interview, or are there troubling discrepancies?

5. Full, honest disclosure is the only way to go. How often have you heard stories in the news about prominent politicians, executives and other headline makers who've been caught in a lie about a degree they hold or honor they received—and asked yourself, "Why would anyone think they could get away with that?" I really don't know the answer to that, but trust me when I say that even unintended discrepancies can come back to bite you. When you post something that's exaggerated or flat-out false on the Internet, you're even more likely to get caught—because your LinkedIn profile and other public posts are there for the entire online community to see.

6. "When we associate a real estate agent with our company, we are allowing that individual to leverage our brand and its 110-year legacy." If Chris hires you, your personal and professional reputation is going to reflect the back on the company. Coldwell Banker takes that very seriously. And consider this: If a company with a 110-year legacy is going to think twice about taking a chance on anyone who

could tarnish its well-established legacy, what about a startup company that's just beginning to build its reputation? Startups have to be even more careful to avoid associating with someone who posts things that are—to use Chris' words—"egocentric, judgmental or polarizing." New businesses that are just starting out already face an uphill battle convincing clients to give their business to a relatively unknown company. In a company with only a handful of employees, even one employee who comes across as unprofessional online can sour a business relationship even before it gets off the ground. Why would a startup take that risk?

How to search for yourself the way employers or clients will search for you.

Now that you understand that employers can (and will) go online to find out more about who you are as a person, ask yourself this: Do you know how employers search for you? And do you really know what they're going to discover? Here are a few do's and don'ts about checking your own results. These are designed to help you better understand how Internet searches might produce different results about you than you might expect, and how you can take steps to control those results.

Don't: Check your online footprint once and then forget about it. Your online results probably aren't changing dramatically every day. But even a small change in the form of a new post made public by you or someone else—or a change in the way search engines decide to rank your results—can make all the difference in affecting your prospects.

Do: Examine your online footprint on a regular basis. We recommend checking it at least once a month (and sometimes once a week), which is why I created a tool called Footprint Friday. This tool reminds (and helps) you to search for yourself online each week in less than 5 minutes. I originally designed this tool for myself but found it so helpful I made it available to others. You can sign up to search for yourself at FootprintFridayTool.com, fill in the relevant information about yourself, and we'll send you an email every Friday with buttons you can click on to obtain a complete picture of your online footprint. This is a great way not only to search the right way—which I'll explain in just a moment— but also to remember to do it, because every week you'll see that email there to remind you.

Don't: Perform a less-than-thorough search. If you only search your first and last name and assume that's all anyone ever sees, you could be missing much of what's in your digital footprint (and giving up too early). Many employers will keep searching to find more relevant information by adding additional search terms to your name.

Do: Try different name and keyword combinations. Footprint Friday offers another important advantage, which is to make it easy to see your personal and professional results from several angles. This is one of my favorite things to demonstrate, because most people are surprised to see how easy it is to find information about people if you go beyond your first and last name.

Start by adding in your middle name, and see what new items pop up. Then start adding in different "keywords." For an individual, keywords include everything from the college or grad school you attended to former companies you've worked for, cities you have lived in and projects you've been associated with. Footprint Friday provides a convenient form you can fill out in five minutes or less with all of these prompts, so every Friday you can search your results using all of these combinations just by pushing the buttons contained in the email. And while you're at it, there are buttons in the report that help you search for "Images," "Videos" and "News" about yourself—all of these will bring up different results.

Don't: View your footprint through your eyes only. I see it all the time—people look at their search-engine results and don't notice much that seems unusual because they understand the context of everything they're looking at. But will everyone else? What about that quirky Facebook club you started five years ago and forgot about after a week? It's still on your profile, and potential employers may not get the joke. All those party pics a friend from college recently dug up and posted—replete with mentions of you holding one of those ubiquitous red plastic cups? How would an employer know if those were from years ago and not last night?

Do: Ask a trusted friend or colleague to go through your profile with you and give you honest feedback. He or she will probably have lots of questions about what they're seeing that will give you a much better idea of what your digital profile is telling your employer. When they ask questions (or make comments), be sure to write them down and listen. Try not to get defensive. Their honest feedback will give you insight into the mind of an employer (or outsider) as to what others think about your "digital first impression."

Digital first impression—that's a phrase to remember. Memorize that concept, post it on your laptop, make it your screensaver or whatever it takes, because I can't emphasize it enough. It's common for people to do a search on you before you even meet. Perhaps they search for you when they have your resume in front of them and are thinking of calling you in for an interview. This person looks impressive, Mr. or Ms. Big might be thinking, but who are they, really? Whom do they know? What do they like to do? Do they seem like someone who's trustworthy, respectful and has a good attitude (etc.)?

So it's actually more than a digital first impression. In many cases, your online footprint might be the first impression (and we all know, you only get one chance to make it). And by the way, don't expect an alert to let you know in advance when they plan to check you out online. As you've probably noticed, the Internet is open for business 24/7, so you always need to be aware of your search results and feel confident that you've done your best to optimize them. This book gives you the tools to do so—but don't wait until you're actively looking for a job or promotion or anticipating a performance review.

Think of it the way you might think of your house or apartment. When you're expecting company, you probably take extra time to clean up before your guests arrive. But what about the times your mother-in-law stops in unexpectedly for a visit? Or a neighbor you've been hoping to ask out for a date comes by to borrow an egg?

If the only times you straightened up, dusted, vacuumed or took out the trash were occasions when you knew company was coming, the unexpected drop-in would be a disaster. You'd have to either stand awkwardly in the doorway trying to block the mess behind you (they're going to see past you anyway—and wonder what you're trying to hide) or just let them in hoping they'll assume you're usually a very neat person who's having an off day. But isn't life easier if you take time regularly to keep the place presentable? Your online footprint is the same way:

You never know when someone's going to check it (and often you'll never know they did).

Even if you do have a little advance warning, it usually takes more than a few minutes to get an accurate picture of your results and even longer to resolve any problem areas you find.

So having a positive digital footprint—like keeping a clean, presentable home—isn't something you achieve once and cross off the list. It's an ongoing process. You always have to stay on top of it, but if you follow the tips in this book and use our free tools like Footprint Friday, it will become second nature to continue to improve it with less and less effort. That way, you'll welcome people searching for you online, confident they'll find the most positive, interesting and genuine aspects of your life that you've worked hard to cultivate.

Are you monitoring your online image?

Register for our FREE Footprint Friday tool to manage your online brand each week in less than 5 minutes.

Visit FootprintFridayTool.com

Chapter 4: Social media posts and strategies that impress employers

---

"If you cannot be positive, then at least be quiet."
— Joel Osteen

Here are some key takeaways from this chapter:

- **Showing your positive, authentic self online goes far beyond making a good impression on potential employers.** You should also care about the impression you're making on current employers, clients, and colleagues who search for you online (or find things online by accident).

- **Always ask yourself: What elements of my life do I want to share with others?** (Hint: The answer is not "everything.") It's okay to be silly and make fun of yourself (not others) online, but if you're venting, being hateful, or sharing personal drama, always call or text a friend instead.

- **Whenever it's appropriate, take a group picture at the end of successful projects.** If it's work related, ask permission first—9 times out of 10 your employer will love it. Be sure to include a sincere THANK YOU to them for the chance to work there and help promote a specific project

---

or client. (If alcoholic beverages are being served, politely ask everyone to leave them out of the photo.)

- **When texting your friends, use all the shorthand or trendy acronyms you want. When posting online, go old-school** and spell out words, use proper grammar, and write like the professional you are.

When an industry leader like Chris Mygatt shares his valuable insight into how Coldwell Banker decides what Realtors would be a good fit for the company—as he does in Chapter Two—here's what you need to remember. It's exactly the same wisdom that applies to how your current employer views you. Again, it's not just potential employers who search for you online when you're an applicant. It's your current employer who might want to give you a more prominent position in the company or give you more responsibility and better pay to go with it. Some of your company's prospective clients will also search for you when they want to know more about the individuals with whom they'll be working—and if they discover something about you on social media that rubs them the wrong way, it doesn't only hurt your relationship with the client (and they'll never tell you why—that's another SOK). It hurts your company's relationship with the client. The result? It comes full circle to damage your upward mobility within that company (and opportunities at other companies that might be looking at you).

Next up are your colleagues—and for many of us, colleagues are the people we're most likely to have a direct relationship with on social media platforms. So every time you post online, you need to think about Sally in the cubicle next to yours, Bob the office gossip, or Catherine, whose work seems to be getting a lot of positive attention from the higher-ups. Maybe you like to think you're above office politics, but if that's your goal, it's all the more important to be thoughtful and positive in your online activities. Your colleagues will respect that, and if they have a positive view of you, your employer will notice. They're more likely to view you as someone who can build consensus and take on roles of leadership.

It's this simple: A negative online image makes you a liability to your employer. Conversely, a positive online image can make you more valuable.

Now is a good time to take a step back and explain what it really means to be Light, Bright, and Polite®, and why I consider it a starting point to maintain a great online reputation—one that's good for all areas of your life, including your career.

So here's the secret:

Always ask yourself: What elements of my life do I want to share with others?

- **Light:** Positive and grateful
    - It's okay to be silly, just keep it self-deprecating, make fun of yourself (not others).
- **Bright:** Be smart and think first, should this be a tweet or a text?
    - Be your authentic self, but when you are venting,

---

call or text a friend. Don't write a public post. Your employer will see it.

- **Polite:** Are you proud if this ends up on your boss' desk tomorrow?
  - o Even though you might not get feedback immediately, this may end up in your annual review. By that time, it may be too late.

This is not a set of catchphrases. It's a philosophy that may protect you over the long term by encouraging you to think outside of the moment.

The goal of this chapter is to show you how to put your best foot forward for your employer. Living (online and off) by these recommendations can help you develop professionally within your current or future job, hone your own "brand" as a professional and be a part of the positive image your company wants to project.

We're also going to give professionals some tips on how to get ahead of the crowd by using social media as well as old-school techniques with new digital tools.

Lisa Cochrane, Former Senior Vice President of Marketing at Allstate Insurance Corp., gives young professionals the three following pieces of advice:

1) Be authentic and professional.

First, be authentic—let your real self shine through—but think about and curate what the public can see when they search you. Not everything about your authentic self is for public viewing. For example, you could make your Facebook private but strategically choose a few posts and photos to set as "public." Make two or three of your best profile pictures public (great shots of you, you in an interesting place, doing something in the community, with your family, etc.) and any posts about career interests, school, volunteering, your most recent work (if you're an artist, writer, etc.), press clips, etc. If someone is searching to find information about you online, this is a good way not to seem totally closed off and still control exactly what you want people to know about you.

Always consider an outsider's perspective before you share socially or voice an opinion. Others don't know you as well as your personal network and may judge you out of context.

Tactical Tip: To improve your online results to strengthen your company's image: If you're active in nonprofit and/or professional organizations, ask to be given a bio on their website or spotlighted in their blog as a core volunteer or member. Having another organization speak for your performance is more valuable than self-promotion.

2) Are you a good writer? Show it online.

I always look for good communication skills. Although the world has changed and texting and email allow for a more informal and conversational writing style, there's still no replacement for good, old-fashioned English that is used well. Use correct spelling, grammar, and punctuation. While "OMG" and "ROFL" work in your personal network, they don't transfer well into the professional world.

Tactical Tip: Choose your words wisely—less is sometimes more.

3) Show you've thought about your future.

Consider using separate social media handles for publishing personal and professional content. Having a public Twitter and LinkedIn where you share industry-relevant content and ideas (don't go overboard, choose wisely) will demonstrate your passion and knowledge in your field(s).

If you deliver a notable speech or performance that somebody captured on video (think about this in advance and make sure you have a designated videographer), upload it to YouTube and make it searchable with your name. As always, make sure your employer is okay with this first.

Lisa makes some great points that will help young professionals to shine online.

Here are some of Josh's activities that employers tend to like to discover on social media:

1. **Volunteering to help others** (in non-political activities) like working at a dog shelter, assisted living home, hospital, etc.

2. **Being involved in subjects you are passionate about** that help others or help you grow as a person. That could include running for a cause, traveling, building cars, sailing, cooking, playing an instrument or other hobbies that make you more well-rounded (and may have a great

story).

3. **Helping to organize events that relate to your industry.**
   If you're not already plugged in with a professional
   association, don't just show up—ask how you can help.
   This will make you stand out with others in your field (and
   lead to great group photo opportunities for social media.)
   One of my favorite things to do at a networking event is to
   volunteer to check people in at the front desk. This helps
   the event organizer and allows me to meet everyone in
   the room while also giving back.

**Here are some activities you might consider keeping off
your social media:**

1. Photos of you holding alcohol at a party

2. Selfies of you sticking your tongue out (or flipping off the
   camera in a casual manner)

3. Inside jokes that are crude in nature

4. Photos of you at a famous landmark being disrespectful

5. Sharing photos of your friends being irresponsible

6. Illegal actions (or skirting the rules) and thinking it's funny
   to share

7. Complaining about a past job, boss, or work-related
   situation

8. Bragging online about actions that could negatively
   impact your future (or others')

9. Not being appreciative of good people, situations, and
   opportunities

10. Bragging about getting away with lying to a former
    employer or cheating them out of work time

Never forget to thank your employer and those who help you accomplish your goals.

When I became a political candidate I needed to surround myself with trustworthy people who also looked out for my image. I was fortunate that one of my closest friends accepted my request to volunteer as my campaign manager in 2009 when I was running for city council in Hermosa Beach. Her name is Jessica McIntyre and she used to work in HR at Nestle, then GoPro and now she's onto another big brand as she climbs the ladder in her career.

I trusted Jessica with my image on the campaign trail and she always made great decisions. When impressing employers, Jessica recommends:

"It's always a good idea when posting something on social media to compliment the people you work for. Whenever you can sincerely thank your employer/team for giving you the chance to work on a project, you're usually going to impress them when (not if) they find it on social media."

Ryan Holmes, CEO of Hootsuite (the largest social media platform in the world), says: "Social media is no longer just for sharing cute pet photos with your friends. In the right hands, it's a powerful tool—your social media profiles can mean the difference in finding and keeping a job. Use social networks like LinkedIn to create a professional and attractive brand online and woo prospective employers. The great thing about social media is that you can control what others see and know about you. So make sure you use networks to your advantage by building a professional personal brand that is, well, professional."

Do employers like side projects?

The answer to this depends entirely on the nature of the project and the way it's presented. If you have a side project that's blatantly entrepreneurial in nature (i.e., you're marketing products or services online), it will just confuse people, including clients of your company. Wait, is this the same Chris who is my account manager at Wonka Industries, and now he's selling a new dog food dispenser he invented? Your employer, meanwhile, might assume you're just biding your time at your current job until your side project takes off. And I can't say it enough—your employer may never say a word to you about it. But conversely, keeping your social media activities focused on your future goals and career paths will open up opportunities you never saw coming and never thought possible.

That is not to say you have to appear on social media as if you have no outside life or interests. Again, authenticity is an asset. But before you start posting about a new project, consider the following:

1. Does the project help others?

As part of a fundraiser, a local public-radio station asked a friend of mine, who is an artist on the side, to design a limited-edition holiday ornament as a featured thank-you gift to donors. He first talked with his employer, got approval and then went ahead to design the art piece.

He took the opportunity to use every social media account he had to thank the station for letting him participate and encourage friends to make a pledge to the station, which relies on donations to provide a public service.

His day job as an editor for corporate publications has little to do with the visual art he makes on the side. But his employer loved to hear about the opportunity up front, to find out he was using his talents for a good cause—and showing gratitude in the process. One tweet read, "Had fun on air with @WBHM yesterday! Support pub radio & get limited edition print with my custom-designed ornament."

So if you have time for side projects, it's great to highlight how your efforts help the community. It's the opposite of showing off if you're helping others with your skills.

2. Why is getting approval so important?

For one, it shows that you understand and respect the fact that your online activities can affect your employer. The unfortunate reality is that many employees neglect even to consider this. You score points when you demonstrate to your boss or human resources that you see the bigger picture.

But of course, you're not just asking as a formality. There is a chance your employer will not approve of your going public online with a side project—not because they're mean or want to thwart your efforts, but because they have a genuine concern about how it will impact the company.

Maybe you're involved in a group or cause that is politically sensitive for your employer or clients. There may be a conflict of interest you're unaware of. If you don't ask, you'll never know—and once you've posted something that hurts your company, the damage is done. You can delete the post, but you have no idea who's already seen it, and you can't control what they'll do with the information (including complaining to your employer).

So by all means, ask before you post about a side project. If there is a conflict, you might be able to work out a compromise by tweaking the message in a way that avoids the conflict. Either way, you'll all be on the same page, and you might be saving yourself from an embarrassing or even career-damaging social media mistake.

What top employers look for in employees' and job candidates' social media

My friend Julie Mossler is the Head of Brand and Global Marketing at Waze, an innovative mapping application acquired by Google. She offers professionals the following advice:

- **Always weed those old posts!** "Younger you" was cool and knew everything, or so you thought at the time. Now, the "new you" knows even more. What seemed like a good thing to share two years ago may not jibe with who you are as a person or professional anymore. There is no harm in deleting stale content when it doesn't fairly represent who you are today, especially when it can help you strengthen your career with your employer, colleagues, and clients.

- **Consistency is key.** If your tweets are peppered with

arguments with friends or a significant other, one might assume your judgment is poor. No one wants to read your drama online! It makes me consider, Will you do that when you represent our brand, too? There's a level of your personal life the Internet doesn't need to know about—learn that comfort zone, and stay within the box.

Posting tips for young professionals

Camille Marquez, who joined our company when she was still a senior in college, is now an account manager for the Los Angeles office of Refinery29, a popular online media lifestyle platform. As a self-proclaimed millennial, she's grown up as part of the social media generation and sets a great example for being Light, Bright, and Polite® as well as completely authentic online. She's also a great example of how much employers like to find potential hires who are making a conscious effort (even if they make it look easy) to manage their online reputation. When we first met Camille, she was doing phone sales in college. She had little experience in what we do, but we took a chance on her primarily because of how positive she was online. It reinforced my view that online identities rarely lie about the true person, because Camille was terrific—every bit as LBP, genuine, well-rounded, thoughtful, full of gratitude, and dedicated to everything she put her mind to as she appeared in her posts. And apparently others agreed: after she graduated from college, she went on to work at the world's largest digital ad agency—OMD—running digital strategy for the Nissan national account.

Camille offers her peers a few tips that she employs in

constructing her own digital media footprint, most often using Instagram and Snapchat as her platforms of choice.

- **As long as your phone/device/laptop are on, you're always representing your company**—whether it's 8 in the morning or 10 at night. "You're working all the time," Camille says. "Especially since we're always on our phone, we're always connected in a way to our company and our job—there's really no distinction anymore. I think you need to be able to represent your company all the time."

- **Be transparent about your whereabouts, because if you misrepresent how you spend your time, social media will "out" you.** "Millennials these days have a hard time distinguishing between work relationships and friendships. You can be friends with your co-workers and even your boss—but if you call in sick and go to Disneyland or the beach, and post something about it, it's very easy for someone who works with you to find it. So if you and your boss really are friends, you're putting them in an awkward position where they have to talk to you about it or even fire you if it's something really bad."

- **Be authentic, but be strategic in your posts.** "I look at my Instagram kind of like a pattern," Camille says. "I might have a post with my friends, and then the next post is me with family, and then maybe the next is one where I'm doing a hobby or working out or something else, so people see that I'm well-rounded. I think a lot of people only post themselves hanging out with their friends or going out or partying, but I think it's really important to look at your Instagram feed in total and say, 'If I didn't know this person, what would I think they like to do?' For me personally, I think if you look at my Instagram page, you can see that I like to hang out with my friends, but I also like to be with my nieces and nephews, I like to work out, I like to do a lot of different things. So you paint a picture of yourself on social media. It's easy to do—you just have to be strategic about it."

Here are a few examples from Camille's Instagram feed that demonstrate how she uses social media to shine online:

Since having close family relationships is a big part of Camille's life, she's proud to show that side of herself on social media.

Any day is a great day to spend with my mom!

Camille loves to show her fun side with friends in a way that's both authentic and tasteful. (Note that she mentions wine tasting in Malibu, but no one is intoxicated or showing off drinks—and she chose a picture that makes everyone look good.)

Malibu wine tasting kind of Saturday 🍷

Another huge part of Camille's life is hanging out with her family, including her young nieces and nephews. This is a great shot she took after they came back from the pumpkin patch.

How awesome are my niece and nephew? Thanks for a great day picking pumpkins! You made my weekend!

Payal Kadakia, a successful businesswoman who founded the popular fitness studio app ClassPass, was so impressed with Camille she took a selfie with her and reposted it on her own Instagram (below). Note how Camille shows her gratitude to Payal and admiration for how she helps others through her company.

"Success comes from being happy." —Payal Kadakia 🙏 Today I met @payal222, CEO and Founder of ClassPass. This company has truly changed my life and I am forever grateful for the impact it's made on my overall health & happiness. She's truly my biggest inspiration.

Payal then reposted the image of Camille—and gave a shout-out to Camille's employer, Refinery29, which her boss loved. It makes Camille a great company ambassador just by doing something she already loves.

"Great speaking @Refinery29 today! Best part was meeting one of our members who is almost at her 500th class!!! @classpass #goals"

payal222

Past Classes (486)

REFINERY29

♥ 39 likes

payal222 Great speaking @refinery29 today! Best part was meeting one of our members who is almost at her 500th class!!! @classpass #goals

Camille enjoys a variety of things in her life—hanging out with friends, family, work, hobbies and talents—and her social media reflects that. Camille's posts from Disneyland shows her silly and social side, and they're always Light, Bright, and Polite®. Her posts mention fun, light topics—nothing she'd be embarrassed for her Mom (or her boss) to see.

Minnie Mouse cousins ❤ It's a great day to visit Disneyland.

This one image captures so much—Camille doing something healthy that she's passionate about—exercising (in a beautiful setting), spending time with friends, and showing

off the city she loves (Los Angeles). It also changes things up a bit by focusing on all of the above instead of herself—visually and in the caption.

There's no other place I'd rather call home.

Josh's formula for posting

This is the formula I use for volunteer or other outside-of-work posts. Once again, please get your employer's approval before sharing anything that might change your online image.

Group photo steps for success

At the end of every group project, I like to take a picture with the entire group. If you're working on a group project at the office, ask if you can take an approved group photo with your peers and/or a customer/client.

In 2013 I launched an aviation program for kids. It has helped to introduce about 3,000 kids to planes and pilots over the past few years. Each child gets to sit in a plane for 5+ minutes, play with the steering wheel (yoke) and take a photo with a real pilot. At the end of the day, I ask our 10-20 volunteers to take a group photo. This is what it looks like.

Thank you to the 20 volunteers that helped us give 400+ kids the chance to sit in a real airplane today and meet a pilot at the Santa Monica Airport.

I got my career started by hosting networking events. Who says photos need to be boring? Here's me getting everyone together and snapping a few photos. This is a pic I posted the next day of the event.

Tactical Tip: Your current (and future) employers are more inclined to approve of you posting about their company when you give a sincere THANK YOU to them for the chance to work there (and helping them to promote a specific project or client). Use caution, though, because once you post something about an employer, you are always and irrevocably tied to that company. Anything else that you post, even if it is personal and has nothing to do with a work situation, will reflect on your employer and their company. For that reason, make sure that you are Light, Bright, and Polite® in everything you do online so that there is not a chance of you embarrassing your employer and getting yourself into a lot of trouble with them. Also, it's a great idea to check in with your employer to ask them if posting about them is okay.

Along the same idea, take a great group photo at the beginning of a business networking event or social hour, which happens to be when most people look their best and most energetic. Make sure everyone puts down (or hides) any beverages, or red cups, and let the photo highlight how social the event is. Have everyone squeeze together with genuine smiles and look directly at the camera.

Social media FAQ's

Will I just look like every other employee if I follow your advice?

Chances are, probably not. People are so different that 99% of the people who read this book will put my formula into effect in different ways. Unfortunately, some won't use these techniques at all. If you do use these techniques to shine online, you are likely going to use the formula in a way that highlights your unique take on a project in a positive way. If you are your authentic self (while being full of gratitude and positivity) you will be very unique.

Is there any risk of getting in trouble for sharing company secrets?

Yes! Be sure to always ask your employer before sharing anything work related on social media. Though well meaning, your post could inadvertently share information the company wasn't yet ready to make public. So by all means, please, ask permission before you take a picture of your group or project. Nine times out of 10, your employer will say "Sure, no problem," especially if you clarify what the picture is for and where it's going to be shared. When in doubt, don't share unless you have permission. Never share any company secrets. Instead, only allude to what is already public information and highlight the positive side of the story. Really, your post should be more about the group photo than about bragging with details.

How do I get people to want to take photos with me for this?

All you need to do is ask them. Most of the time, people will be happy to. Consider using the following phrase, "Do you mind taking a group photo with me that we could share on our blog to highlight this project?" Or, "Employer, may I take a group photo that we can share on our company Facebook page? I will take the initiative to make it look nice and do something nice for the company." Or, "Can we take a group photo that highlights the client?" or "Employer, can we take a picture with the client to say thanks to them for working with us?" The employer will typically say yes.

Then, find someone else to snap the photo from the other side of the room (selfies aren't great for group photos).

Your employer will think it's great that you're sharing their information in a positive way (with permission). Assure them that you won't share any confidential information. Just about every employer will say yes to that because it's effortless, positive advertising for their group. Group photos can be a part of almost every one of your projects.

Chapter 5: Social networks that help you shine online

"I find that the harder I work, the more luck I seem to have."
—Thomas Jefferson

Key takeaways from this chapter:

- **Gone are the days when employers trusted your PDF resume** or Microsoft Word resume without looking you up online.

- **It's good to have a thick, relevant history on LinkedIn** that others can discover and point to as your professional home base online.

- **Get a classy photo.** Keep in mind that since the printed version of your resume doesn't have a picture on it, you need a clear, classy photo of yourself online that others can use to quickly identify you.

- **You want to own and control the first page of search results others see when they look for you online**, and since Google Plus and YouTube are owned by Google (which will nudge their content to the top), those are great places to start.

- **Build a personal website.** If you build a personal website, you can add projects, resumes, and volunteer work to help keep your results fresh.

- **Let some photos get discovered.** If your security settings are set to friends only, or friends of friends only, consider making a select few of your best pictures public so that your profile is the first to be discovered instead of someone else's by mistake.

- **It's important to have a clear, professional email address.** You will never grow out of your email address when it contains your full name.

- **Consider creating a clear and concise bio** that puts your best foot forward online (without giving away too much personal information).

I get a lot of questions from people that ask, "Okay, I've used your techniques to get an accurate picture of my Google results, and there are some aspects I don't like. So how do I fix negative/obsolete posts that show up under my name on Google?" My answer is always the same: Create positive content to push the bad stuff down. This is a highly effective first step toward owning the first page of your Google results.

To do this, you will need to set up and activate several social networks that will help you push bad posts down and float the good stuff to the top.

In this chapter, I'm going to outline several of the social media networks that will help you to push your best content to the top of Google and shine online.

Here's a list of my favorite networks that I suggest you consider spending time on:

LinkedIn best practices

It's a very good idea to spend a lot of time filling out all of your LinkedIn profile items with clear information that describes your work history and past projects. This is a professional form of social media that is discovered first by Google. I can't overstate the importance LinkedIn plays in creating a first impression online because it shows up on the first page of online search results when people are looking for you.

LinkedIn is the future of your resume—and so much more. For those who are in the job market, gone are the days when employers trusted your PDF or Microsoft Word resume without looking you up online. Nowadays they take your resume and compare it to LinkedIn to match a face to a name.

If you are trying to build your client list or move up the ranks within your existing company, the same principles apply. A business card used to provide basic contact information for people to get in touch. Now, it's a piece of paper your new prospect (or even future employer) will take straight to the computer tomorrow to find out who you really are—and if they want to do business with you and your company.

So it's very important your LinkedIn profile conveys the image you want it to. It's good to have a thick, relevant history on LinkedIn that employers, higher-ups within your company, colleagues and clients can discover and point to as your professional home base online.

Under each description for projects and work experience in LinkedIn, here's my technique that will help you stand out from the crowd:

The first line of your job description should include a one-sentence description of what the organization or business does in its industry. This will provide outsiders with a useful context. For example, I wrote under Disney Studios: "Disney is the largest media and entertainment conglomerate in the world with revenues of $36.1 billion."

The second section of your description should include what your role was at the company or organization. It can be bulleted or paragraph style and can be thankful in nature. For example, I wrote: "Disney/Buena Vista Home Entertainment was a wonderful experience for me. I worked closely with seven departments and managed all areas of DVD projects from start to finish. My boss would set the stage for production, and I would assist in all meetings to track creative, operations, financials, promotions and media. I negotiated with outside vendors and had a blast winning over people in other divisions. Disney was a wonderful place to start my career and I often refer back to this job in my public speaking."

Below your job description, you have the opportunity to insert bullets or a special quote from the employer they may have written to you in a letter of recommendation. One of the best forms of sales is having someone else say nice things about you. As an example, here's what I put in my third section:

Here's an excerpt from my former boss at Disney that I put on my LinkedIn profile:

"Josh is eager, persistent, positive and, well, people just like him. Even now, when Josh drops by for a visit employees of every level pop out of their offices to say hello. Josh's people skills are awe inspiring. And best of all, like Superman, he uses his power for good, not evil. He has renegotiated deadlines, coaxed extra effort out of vendors, wheedled talent into extraordinary PR—and always, the people who work with Josh feel lucky, happy and relaxed. That's the magical part. Josh's attitude is relentlessly sunny. Throw him a moody executive, harsh feedback, an insurmountable "No" and Josh rebounds effortlessly. His refusal to respond personally to professional setbacks helps to keep the entire team focused on the business objectives during tense and potentially contentious negotiations."

—Lisa Clements, Former Director of Marketing at Walt Disney Studios

Tactical Tip: While we're on the subject of LinkedIn, I'll let you in on a little-known secret: It's not only employers, potential employers or anyone considering working with you who look at your profile. Many bloggers and journalists rely on LinkedIn as a fast and easy way to find sources for stories. If you want to be the professional in your industry who they call for quotes, a strong presence on LinkedIn can move you to the top of their list—and in many cases they will quote verbatim from the information you've provided to tell their readers who you are. It's imperative that what they see on LinkedIn—and then repeat—is correct.

Learn more of my LinkedIn tips by watching a video at MediaLeaders.com/book to get an exclusive set of tips you can use to set up your digital resume.

Google Plus steps for success

Google Plus is owned by Google and its results are given an unfair advantage over other social media accounts to be displayed on the first page of your search results.

When someone searches for you online, you want to own and control the first page of the search results they see, and since Google Plus is owned by Google, it's a great place to start.

If you have a Gmail address, you can quickly activate your Google Plus account with just a few clicks.

Although HR managers and college admissions use this

network less than LinkedIn, Google Plus will allow you to get discovered in Google's search results (and image results) much quicker (since it has an unfair advantage in Google's algorithm).

You're probably thinking that you don't have time to post on yet another account. Don't worry—all you need to do is post to your Google Plus page once every few months with an image and message. Most of the time this can be done from your phone and be a repeat of your best Instagram posts.

It's wise to use a profile photo and bio that is similar to the one you use on LinkedIn, Twitter, Facebook and any other networks you are on so you can easily be discovered online by those that search for you.

In addition, your Google Plus profile should display links to all of your other networks so Google can link them to your "digital identity" and use that info to serve up the most relevant results for those searching for you. This will help you to combat the problem of other people (who might share your name, or a name close to yours) being displayed in your search results.

Your Google Plus account should be tied to your Gmail address so you can get updates in your inbox in case you have little time to check this network.

Google Plus Tactical Tip: Write captions in the third person. Since very few people use Google Plus, this is a great place to use photo captions in a way that helps change your Google results. To do so, consider including your full name in captions that describe photos. This will help to adjust your Google Image results. Example: "Thank you to the Orange County Animal Shelter for letting Josh Ochs and his friends volunteer to help 7 dogs find homes this weekend." On Instagram, it would feel very awkward to talk about yourself in the third person while your friends are following you. However, Google loves it when you talk about yourself in the third person because it uses those keywords to adjust your Google rankings. Since very few people are on Google Plus, this is a great place to use your full name (even if it feels unusual at first).

Personal website steps for success

When people search my name online as "Josh Ochs" it's my goal to have Google quickly be able to recognize my personal website as the authority with those keywords. This is why I purchased JoshOchs.com and have slowly been adding content to it over the last several years.

Buying your own website is a great way for you to quickly own something online that can eventually help you control the first page of your search results. This becomes a part of your identity on the web. Here you can start your own portfolio of accomplishments and update it on a regular basis.

Whether it's athletics, social work, volunteering, etc. you can post photos and videos to your own website so that search engines will put you above other random results.

To see how we set up our sites, visit MediaLeaders.com/book and register this book to watch a free set of videos on WordPress.

What domain should you buy?

My real first name is Joshua but people call me Josh. Therefore, I bought the domain with the exact spelling that people use to search for me online: JoshOchs.com. If having both names is important to you, you could possibly buy the formal spelling of your name and have it forwarded to the more common spelling.

Although you want to use the domain that includes the spelling of your name that people will search for, it's also smart to buy the misspelling of your name (in my case I have a last name that is misspelled often). As an example: I own JoshOaks.com in addition to JoshOchs.com. I direct the traffic from the misspelled domain to the correctly spelled domain. It's an investment to have people discover me and not get lost. If you visit JoshOaks.com you will be instantly forwarded to JoshOchs.com.

Once you have your website built, try to add projects, resumes, and volunteer work at least once per month. The more often you share relevant, helpful content, the more likely that search engines will see that your website is dynamic and a useful resource for people who are searching for you—which is why they'll be inclined to put it on the first page of your Google results.

Have other people look over your website and provide you with tips so you can make the messaging and pictures tell the best story about your accomplishments. The site doesn't have to be very fancy; the story of your accomplishments and portfolio are the most important parts.

Tactical Tip: Here are some free/low-cost places to host your personal website: Blogger.com, SquareSpace.com, Wordpress.com, Wix.com, Shopify.com or Weebly.com. Also, consider visiting domains.google.com to buy your domain name. They are my trusted source.

Facebook steps for success

Have a Facebook profile even if you think it is outdated. Managers are still using Facebook to look for you. Employers do have time to look for you online, and you want to use it to stand out in a positive way.

This is a great place for you to post photos and descriptions of jobs and volunteer work you've done.

Don't be lazy online just because you don't think people will find your posts. Trust me: if it's online, people will find it—and you had better be proud of it, because when it does get discovered, it's either going to be the up button on the elevator of your career or it's going to be the down button.

Every post will either take you up or down.

Use your real name as someone would spell it in an interview.

If your security settings are set to friends only, or friends of friends only, consider making a select few of your best pictures public so that your profile is the first to be discovered instead of someone else's by mistake.

Keep it clean by not letting people automatically tag you in photos without your approval. Also, don't let people automatically check you in online at venues since it may not be somewhere that makes you shine online. Even if you're at a simple coffee shop, your friend may check you in, and suddenly your profile might read: "I'm at Big Daddy's Beans!" which might not seem appropriate to an outsider who could misunderstand the venue's name.

Should you set your Facebook page to friends only? If you're trying to impress your employer or clients, you might consider cleaning up any inappropriate photos on Facebook so you can make it public and have many of your volunteer activities and accomplishments displayed on your profile.

Even if your Facebook is hidden, make sure you are making Light, Bright, and Polite® posts. Anything can be found on the Internet (and your well-meaning best friends could always comment on/share something that gets your photos discovered).

Instagram steps for success

Create a distinct, clear bio on Instagram with a username that is easy for search engines to match to your real name (Look at my profile @JoshOchs or http://instagram.com/JoshOchs as an example on Instagram). Be very clear about who you are and use the same profile picture that you did for every other site. This will help to connect the dots among all your profiles.

Since Instagram is so widely used, it's easy for several profiles to come up under your name. Having a uniform picture and clear bio will identify you and minimize the chance you'll be confused with someone else.

Instagram can be part of a well-balanced reputation across several networks. As always, make sure everything you post on Instagram is Light, Bright and Polite®.

Should you set your Instagram to private? If you want positive images, volunteer activities, etc. to be discovered by your employer/supervisor/clients, you might consider keeping it public. Just be sure to clean up any inappropriate photos on your account first—and consider having a friend look through your profile and tell you what images you should delete before making your Instagram public.

Also note, if you share most of your private Instagram photos on Twitter (and your Twitter isn't private) then you're really making your Instagram account public. It's very easy for someone to visit your Twitter account and search through your Instagram photos to circumvent the privacy settings.

Your reputation could possibly spill over into these other networks.

YouTube steps for success

Since YouTube is owned by Google, it is given an unfair advantage in search results. Google knows that people love video, and that's why videos will usually appear on the first page of search results in a query.

It's a good idea to tie your YouTube account to your Google Plus name so you can use one login to control them all.

Provide a link in your YouTube profile that links to your Google Plus profile so Google can see that you're starting to weave your online web.

If you have projects or videos of you volunteering, you might consider asking a friend if the content would be a good fit for an employer or your company's clients to discover online. If so, then consider putting them on your YouTube account as a public video so you can build out this very important profile. Every Mac and PC comes with some free video editing software that will let you lightly edit the clips and add an introduction title to explain the video. This ensures that your videos tell the right story on YouTube.

Don't flood your YouTube account with videos to entertain your friends. Instead, keep it Light, Bright, and Polite® in each video and make sure to add value for those who might watch the video. As an example: If you Google "Josh Ochs Jeep" you will find one of my most popular YouTube videos where I share with people how to repair their headlights in their Jeep Grand Cherokee. It has received thousands of views and lots of comments. This video is something I'm okay with my clients discovering, since it shows that one of my hobbies is being handy and I had a good time creating a thoughtful solution that can help other car owners. This small project helps me build my professional portfolio as I use it in marketing meetings with clients as an example they can use to help their customers in their videos.

Gmail address steps for success

Now that you're a professional—even if you have a separate work email—take a moment to evaluate your Gmail address. Is it simple, clean and easy for people to remember?

Perhaps many years ago you set up an email address that contains your nickname but doesn't sound very professional. Now would be a great time to set up an email address with this format: [First name] + [Last name] @gmail.com or [first name] + [middle initial] + [last name]@gmail.com. Gmail is viewed as an email system used by professionals and will be well received if the address contains a name that clearly identifies you.

You will never grow out of your email address when it contains your full name. However, you will quickly grow out of an email address that contains a childhood username. As an example, my childhood email address was Swimmer174@aol.com. As the captain of the high school swim team, this seemed appropriate at the time. However, I have since changed my email address to be more like [First name] + [Last name] @Gmail.com. Not only was my old email address short-sighted, it was also difficult for people to find my email address when they opened a new message and typed in "Josh Ochs" since Swimmer174 wasn't picked up by autosuggest.

It's important to have a clear, professional email address.

There's no need to email everyone alerting them that you changed your email address. Look carefully in the settings of Gmail and give it permission to log into your old email account automatically so it can download any new messages every day to your new account for free. Then, you can begin replying to everyone with your new address and everything will funnel into your new Gmail address seamlessly.

As an added benefit, when your employer wants to send something to you online, whether it's a presentation, worksheet, product, or document, you can recommend, "Please share it with me using Google Docs. Here's my Gmail account, firstname.lastname@gmail.com." If this address is anything other than a clear description of your identity, then they may frown upon it. They're really going to like being able to contact you through a professional email identity that matches your full name.

Twitter steps for success

Consider creating a clear and concise bio that puts your best foot forward online (without giving away too much personal information). Feel free to put some light humor in the bio so people can see your fun self shine through. Mention your favorite movie or song, but make sure it's positive. Keep the bio about your interests and professionally friendly, casting yourself in the brightest light, and make it authentic. Perhaps it could sound like this: "I'm a dad of 2, a Dodgers fan and my wife wishes I would give up the drums."

Another good example with some self-deprecating humor might be: "Web developer, proud father of 2 and learning how to not burn grilled cheese sandwiches."

Here's an example of a professional: "Brand manager and runner. Guilty pleasure: the Bachelor/Bachelorette."

If you want to own your first page of Google results, make sure you use your real name and that it is spelled in a similar manner to how you expect your employer or clients to search for you online. This will help your Twitter handle reach the first page of your search results.

Let me use myself as an example: My profile name is "Josh Ochs" (the way someone would search for me) and my username is @JoshOchs (making it easier for search engines to see me as the real Josh Ochs and making it easy for web users to make the connection). This ensures that my Twitter handle will come up on the first page during a search for

"Josh Ochs" on Google or Bing.

Here's a few things to consider NOT doing on Twitter:

Be aware that Google is great at connecting the dots between names. Even if your username is @iHeartBeingDrunk, the search engines will be able to connect the dots sometimes and pull up your profile on a search under your name. Make sure your username is something that is positive and something you'll be proud for your employer to find, because they will.

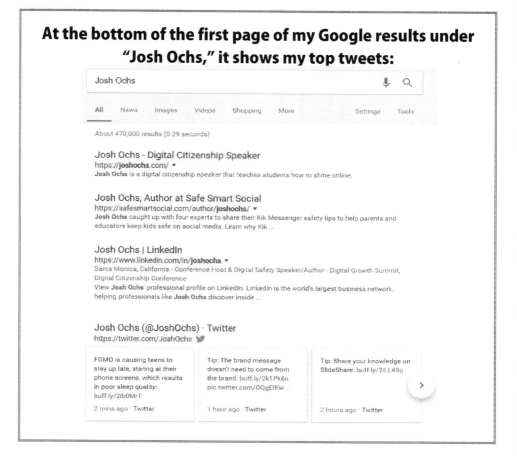

At the bottom of the first page of my Google results under "Josh Ochs," it shows my top tweets:

Also, when someone searches for Josh Ochs, before they press "return", Google suggests four other search results in the search box. They suggest "Josh Ochs Instagram," "Josh Ochs Media Leaders" and a few others. This shows users what to search for to find me.

Some might say, "Aren't you upset that Google is telling people how to find your personal social media profiles?"

Every photo I share is one that I'm proud for all of my clients, my employer and my family to see. My social media accounts are a resume of fun activities that make me a more approachable professional. I hear from clients all the time that the photo of my nephew in an In-N-Out Burger hat is adorable. To find that picture, they had to search for me and look through many of my other photos. They all must be positive and full of gratitude, because clients are watching.

What should I share on Twitter?

Twitter is a great place to share some of your most positive Instagram photos that create a portfolio of your accomplishments. Also, it's a great place to share positive quotes that are inspirational to others. Be careful not to share overly dramatic quotes.

Are you monitoring your online image?

Register for our FREE Footprint Friday tool to manage your online brand each week in less than 5 minutes.

Visit FootprintFridayTool.com

Chapter 6: How to express yourself while managing your online image

---

"Life is 10% what happens to you and 90% how you react to it."
—Charles R. Swindoll

Here are some key takeaways from this chapter:

- **No one's online sharing habits are perfect.** We all give into the temptation from time to time to share harmless jokes (as long as they're not making fun of others) or just pictures of our dog/cat/guinea pig doing something funny. But posts like these ought not crowd out your purposeful posts that show off your fun side along with your professional and grateful side—the kind you want to be discovered by your employer.

- **Learn from other people's social media mistakes and successes.** On any given day, people in your own social media circle are posting great pictures, announcements, etc. full of gratitude and positivity—while others may be busy venting about annoying clients. Seeing real-life examples is a great reminder of how your own posts make an impression on others.

- **If you're not sure something you're about to post is appropriate, it's probably not.** At the very least, sleep on it. (a) I always recommend a private text over a tweet if a topic is too heated for public consumption, and (b) you'll probably have a better perspective tomorrow (or in an hour or two). But once you post it, it's out of your hands.

- **Be careful showing a good time online.** Don't use social media to show off the great time you're having Vegas, at Mardi Gras or in any setting that undermines your professional credibility. Are you entitled to a personal life? Absolutely. Should you post pictures where you appear visibly intoxicated or just plain obnoxious on Facebook, Instagram or anywhere else? No.

You might have noticed by now that I use the word "authentic" a lot. The reason for this is that when groups invite me to come speak about how to shine online and avoid damaging your reputation, this is a common concern I hear: "Josh, we understand what you're saying about creating a positive digital image. But what fun is it if we have to be fake online?"

Yet if you hear me speak, watch any of my video blogs or look at my websites, you will never, ever see or hear the word "fake." In fact, being fake usually backfires, because people can see through it.

Instead, I'm assuming your authentic self is a lot like the rest of us (including me)—a mix of the good, the bad and the quirky. But that's the beauty of social media. You get to choose what to share (or not) about yourself and your life. I just want you to choose wisely.

This chapter will show you how to express yourself and still avoid offending others, causing trouble at work or revealing private details you'll later regret.

Before we start, I want to say that it's totally healthy to want to vent. Sometimes social media seems like the fastest, easiest place to do it. But while you should vent to someone, you have better options. Pick up the phone, call a friend, text your buddy or go to coffee with someone. Venting is totally acceptable as a text (to a friend) but maybe not always as an Instagram/Facebook post that might be seen by others.

Think of your online sharing like a healthy diet. I don't know about you, but I feel great when I eat healthy. Because of that, I try and eat healthy as often as possible. But even die-hard diet gurus acknowledge that it's not realistic to think you'll eat perfectly all the time. Foods like ice cream, French fries, and potato chips are not the best for us, but they can be awfully tempting, so we indulge from time to time. That's okay within reason. But if you were to eat a bag of cheesy poofs every time you sat down to watch a favorite show, it might undermine your goal of feeling energized (and in shape). So although I cheat a lot when it comes to my eating habits, having a simple plan keeps me on track and somewhat healthy.

Having healthy habits when it comes to self-expression online is similar. Throughout the book, I've identified several examples of ways to create a positive digital footprint. The biggest share of your digital footprint should be as "healthy" as possible, and if it is, then that's what will dominate the first page or two of your Google results. The overall impression you create will be positive and comprised of things you'd want people to discover.

The same goes for social media. If one's goal is for their social media presence to be Light, Bright, and Polite®, helping to advance their career and other goals in life, then they should strive for "healthy" online sharing. But it's also okay to give into one's cravings occasionally to share a relatively harmless gripe about something irritating that happened (being careful not to do so at someone else's expense), post a silly picture of your mother-daughter pedicures, or announce that you just spent an entire afternoon binge-watching "Homeland." Just don't go crazy and let those dominate your social media diet. Your friends will think it's fun in small doses, but if you find yourself posting every random thought that comes into your head, then your best posts—the truly positive, grateful and unique ones that help you shine online—will get lost in the chatter.

We all have to break our social media diet a little to let our authentic self shine through. Just make sure it's positive and full of gratitude.

Do a random check of your Facebook/Twitter/other news feeds and see what kind of impression others are making. It's amazing what you can learn about the power of using a personal filter just by seeing what others are posting. As you scroll through, make mental notes:

- Is Brandon's post about a big award he won purely self-congratulatory—or does he use the post to thank his employer for the opportunity and thank his family for their support?

- Does Brenda's post about her ex-boyfriend look like something she's going to regret in the morning (and wish she'd just called a friend instead)?

- Did you just learn something about Dylan's political views that make you see him in a different light, either because you personally disagree with him or know that many others will be offended?

- Did Donna post a comment about her day at work that reflects badly on her professionalism, attitude and employer? (i.e. "Clue to parents—if you have four noisy kids, consider getting a sitter when you need to conduct complicated business at the bank.")

I could think of endless examples, but the most important thing to ask is this: **How do other people's posts make you feel about being associated with them?** Usually, it's easy to spot when another person is being mean spirited or offensive online, and it might make you think twice about having them on your news feed. Yet when we're sharing our own information, sometimes it's not so obvious that our own posts might be less than Light, Bright, and Polite®. When it doubt, sleep on it. Whatever irks us today often seems like ancient history tomorrow (or at least a lot less important).

Learn from others' mistakes to build up your own filter.
You might notice that in the above examples of bad sharing, your friends' desire to express themselves was not the problem. It's how and where they decided to share it. After all, Brandon did win an impressive award, and he's excited about

---

it—as he should be. But presenting that information with a healthy dose of gratitude would make a world of difference in the kind of impression the post or tweet has on others. The other sample posts listed above are great examples of self-expression that's better saved for venting to a friend via text, email or phone, and not for public consumption.

So remember your filter and how many people will see the things you share on social media. **And keep in mind that when you put your worst foot forward by appearing angry, gossipy, dramatic, or not having appropriate boundaries, those are the posts people are most likely to share with others.** (And what do you think they'll say when they screenshot Brenda's rant about her ex and forward it to a mutual friend? Probably not, "Wow, can you believe he's dating again?? Poor Brenda!" Unfortunately they're just as likely to say, "Wow, Brenda really needs to get a life. Didn't they break up three months ago??")

On the other hand, if your bad post gets no response, it doesn't mean no one noticed. It's more likely they've quietly taken note of your controversial political views; your poor judgment in oversharing about your personal life; or your inappropriate rant about customers who annoy you. ("The customer is always right" is as true as ever in the digital age. Remember "Donna" in the example above, who complained about having rowdy kids in her workspace? Any mom or dad who's ever had to bring their kids along to the bank and sees that post will take offense at Donna's thoughtlessness.)

10 ways to negatively post about your company/employer

If you want to know exactly how to be called into the HR department, consider following these examples of negative posts:

1. "Annoyed about my boss"
2. "Customers suck sometimes"
3. "Wish I could go home now"
4. "Need a better job"
5. "I hate cubicles"
6. "I'd love an office computer that didn't crash every 10 min"
7. "My office neighbor is so loud on the phone"
8. "Here's a pic of me not giving a _____ at work"
9. "Our legal team is so slow"
10. "This meeting is boring, everyone thinks I'm emailing a client, but I'm looking for party theme ideas on Pinterest."

Texts vs. Tweets

How do you know when something you want to share is more appropriate as a tweet (or other social media post) or a private text? The simple answer is that a tweet is what you want the public to see, and a text is just for one person or a small group of people. Okay, we all get that in theory. In practice, however, people regularly send out tweets with information that would be better shared in private. An article in the online magazine Slate notes that "even criminals can't resist revealing incriminating evidence about themselves sometimes." That's an extreme example, but it's true that a lot of people like to share what they are doing and get feedback.

Why? We are human and need feedback from other people. That's normal. Does that feedback need to come from someone you text or something you tweet? What's going to get the best feedback for you? When you vent/complain online on Facebook, do you notice that sometimes the same 3-5 people comment/like the post? Those are the only people who wanted to give you feedback (though 50-100 more people saw the post or watched the video). When you notice that happening, consider sending those types of posts as private messages instead of public posts.

Josh's Tactical Tip for Getting Feedback

Create a group text message (or email) with your top 2-5 friends and tell them "Hey, was dying to share this on FB but I love you guys the most. Wanted to get your feedback on this. Here's XYZ." Or, you could create a small Facebook messenger group message that links in all of your closest friends. They would love to hear from you and they will give you feedback.

If instead, you give into the urge to post it on social media, you might be oversharing.

So what does all this have to do with your professional life? All of these problems can affect your career as well as your personal life. For instance, if a boss, coworker or client sees that you're posting personal (and indiscreet) details of a bad breakup, it reflects badly on your judgment—and during your next business meeting, the knowledge (which they never asked for) of the state of your love life will detract from their ability to view you as professional. So when in doubt, always keep private info for your texts/phone calls and the positive stuff in a tweet/Facebook post.

How Not to Live a Double Life

Nobody works all the time—nor should they! We all get burned out from time to time. Taking vacations, spending time with friends and family and just relaxing are important for maintaining a healthy work/life balance.

Naturally, these activities tend to make for the best "photo ops." (When's the last time you took a selfie in front of the water cooler in the office break room?) Most of us love to share these photos on social media, too—there's nothing wrong with wanting to show off your wonderful family, friends or even a beautiful backdrop.

But occasionally when you're in vacation mode, it's tempting to forget that all the rules of normal life when it comes to online sharing still apply. That means if there's anything you wouldn't want your employer/clients/colleagues to see, keep it off social media. Maybe you're thinking, "What, am I not entitled to a private life?" Of course. You are fully entitled to a private life—but if you post it on social media, it's no longer private.

Here's a real-life example of the kind of "double life" sharing that drives employers crazy: A 25-year-old teacher goes to celebrate a girls' (or guys') weekend with their besties in Vegas and gets so caught up in the fun they post photos with sexy clothing, poker tables in the background, drinks raised in the air...you get the idea. It's the opposite of how they want to present themselves in their professional environment to students, supervisors and the parents who trust them to be good role models for their kids. That's what many employers mean by having a "double life." If you want to let loose on a big weekend to celebrate your friend's upcoming wedding or whatever the occasion, that's okay—the wildest of the pictures would be terrific for a text message, but not a public social media post. I know this because it happens, and school principals have told me it drives them nuts.

Of course, this is hardly limited to teachers. If you work in a medical environment, for instance, people need to see you as someone with good judgment. If you handle other people's money, it's the same thing. In fact, with pretty much any job you do, customers/patients/clients/parents chose you or your company because there's a certain level of trust.

If you undermine that trust by publicly showing a "double life" online, you're hurting your employer, and that's not a chance they want to take.

The reality is drinking and social media often don't mix. Alcohol impairs your judgment, so if you've been drinking, consider take a break from posting on social media. You can still take all the pictures you want, and if posting them still looks like a good idea in the morning, go ahead—especially if you add an appropriate tagline, i.e., "So excited for my cousin's wedding and the chance to celebrate with her!"

(drinks out of sight for the picture, and you don't appear visibly intoxicated).

I've been known to ask colleagues and friends to set their drinks aside when we are taking a group photo. Oftentimes people who don't know me will ask, "Why? What's wrong with drinking in photos?" Although it may seem overly cautious at the time, it always makes the photo one that my clients and friends are proud of when we decide to post the photo. If someone insists they don't want to set down their drink, that photo might not be the right fit for your social media posts. **I've never heard anyone say "Hey, you don't have any drinks in your hand in that pic. That party must have been boring."** Instead, keeping the drinks out of the photo makes the event look even more exciting because it focuses on the people in the photo and the fun they are having.

It's no coincidence that people whose posts set a positive and authentic tone are the same people who tend to be doing well in their careers and enjoy a good reputation, professionally and privately.

A friend of mine, Janette Rizk, is a great example of creating a positive online reputation that benefits your career. A public relations and social media expert specializing in food, health, and wellness, Janette adopted the tools of presenting her authentic self in a positive light on social media from its earliest days. As a PR professional, she wanted to make sure she understood what works (and doesn't) and how it impacts a person's or brand's reputation. She practices what she preaches, and the work she's put into her digital footprint has served her well both personally and professionally:

Working in PR, I became really aware early on of the perception that social media creates about people. So I've really been conscious of what would come up if someone searched for me online. I want it to convey who I am as a professional and as a person—knowing that brands, employers and others look at that when they're looking to hire or work with you. So I've added things to my LinkedIn profile and purposely connected with a lot of people as a way to create more connections, and that's definitely helped professionally.

So that's one part of it on the professional side. But also on the personal side, I wouldn't want to post something that would offend someone or didn't represent who I am as a person, either. So I think I've just always been pretty careful, just as I would be in life. What people see online is an extension of who you are—and the things I tend to post personally are about family, food and fitness, because those are some of my biggest interests. Those things are really safe, and they also fit into what I do—because the PR work I do with clients mostly centers around food, health and wellness. If I share articles on Twitter, it usually fits into those areas.

But I think it's really, for me, been an extension of what I would convey in any setting. And fortunately, if it shows up positively in my Google search results, it means I'm doing something right. I participate in a lot of industry-related events, and I remember one former client approaching me after a panel discussion was posted online. He said, 'Oh, I saw that video from MediaLeaders.com and want to get your opinion about this topic related to digital marketing.' So it can be a really powerful vehicle for adding credibility and making connections.

It's great advice from a professional who practices what she preaches about using social media wisely. Remember some of the principles she's laid out—not wanting to post anything that would either offend others or misrepresent her beliefs; posting things that she would feel comfortable with in any setting, and using social media to add credibility—and think how they apply to your own online activity.

Are you monitoring your online image?

Register for our FREE Footprint Friday tool to manage your online brand each week in less than 5 minutes.

Visit FootprintFridayTool.com

Chapter 7: Knowing when (and what) to post/send

"There is no wrong time to do the right thing."
—Charles M. Blow

Here are some key takeaways from this chapter:

- **Your right to privacy is a myth—even if you bring your own device to work.** Once you're plugged into the company server, you are using company resources and time. So whether it's your personal laptop or just your smartphone, when at work, treat these devices just as you would treat company-owned equipment. Besides, you never know when your communications, images, searches and more could enter into the company database.

- **Communicate like a professional.** That might sound obvious, but for many, it takes a conscious effort to leave the acronym- or slang-laden language they use with their friends online at the office door. Take care to write clear, concise emails that get the message across while omitting extraneous details. It's worth taking a few extra minutes to put in the effort and review emails for spelling or grammatical errors before hitting "send."

- **Never put anything in writing that you wouldn't be proud for everyone to see.** Email changed workplace communications by making it easy to communicate and store information, even with large groups of people. Yet human error can still wreak havoc.

- **Some emails are just a bad idea.** Rule of thumb: Try to use emails for communication only—not venting, sharing office rumors or stirring up gossip.

Most of this book so far has focused on social media and the ways you can either help or hurt your career with the choices you make on social media platforms.

But what about communications within the office? Today, email and sometimes even texts have taken the place of the "internal office memo." If you're not old enough to remember, the internal memo—an actual sheet of paper either delivered to a single person or distributed office-wide—was often *uber-*formal, and it was understood that it may be seen by more than just its intended audience.

Almost every company has shifted to 100% email, which is so much more easily shared and stored. But along with that comes plenty of room for error, including everything from sloppy writing to those legendary mistakes where an email ends up in the inbox of someone who was never supposed to see it—or maybe lots of people who weren't supposed to see it.

In other words, there are pros and cons to fast and easy communication. This chapter is intended to help you avoid dangerous pitfalls.

Your right to privacy is a myth—even on your own device

Another useful way to remember to keep all of your emails Light, Bright and Polite® is to understand that once you're plugged into the company server, you are using company resources and time. That means your emails aren't really your own. I'm not a lawyer, and employee privacy laws change, so I'm not attempting to give legal advice. The bigger question is, why would you risk sending offensive, insulting or other messages that are inappropriate for work while you're at the office or using office equipment (including hardware you might have been given to bring home)?

The same wisdom applies whether you're using company equipment or your own. That's important to consider for a few reasons.

BYOD—bring your own device—has become a popular trend at several companies in a number of scenarios, including:

1. The company knows you already have a laptop/iPad/phone you could bring from home, and it saves them money by not having to provide one for you. This is especially true for contract workers who might only work in the office for a few months.

2. You might be bringing it anyway—even if you already have an office computer. How many of us carry our phones and/or tablets everywhere we go, including work? You might not consider these to be "work" devices, but chances are you do use them for work at some point. Do you have your work contacts programmed into your

phone, and do clients have access to your "private" number in case something comes up when you're away from the office? That's a prime example of how interchangeable our "work" and "home" devices are. And Internet providers make no distinction when it comes to the content you send and can be discovered.

3. There are pros and cons to BYOD, and some companies have not created formal policies around personal devices being brought into the workplace, making it that much smarter to err on the side of caution. Just because you can send your best buddy a tasteless joke or picture during a lull in the conversation with a client (which you're conducting on your "office" phone line) doesn't mean you should. Your communications, images, searches and more can enter into the company database. Always remember that today's technology is all about sharing, whether you want to share or not. Every device you bring or use in the office carries a ton of information you might believe will stay private—including yours and that of every member of your household who uses your device or communicates with it via the cloud. Imagine being in an important meeting, and your phone begins sending alerts that someone just beat your child's score in an online video game. While hardly devastating, it's still an example of unprofessional elements you might be bringing into your office along with your devices, like a screenshot of a Snapchat that's not intended for public consumption but is stored in your device and could wind up on the office server.

4. So if you're going to bring your own device, take a hard look at it first at home and make sure you know what's on there. Again, always assume that if something could go wrong, it will. You've seen far too many headlines about

people who should have known better damage their valuable reputations by making careless mistakes that lead to private/embarrassing information becoming public. You can't outsmart the technology—you can never know everything, and it's always changing anyway. That's exactly why I'm in this business—to show others exactly how to maintain a positive online reputation they'll be proud for others to see (and will ultimately help them advance in their careers).

The Anatomy of a good email

When just starting out at a company, most people want to get a feel for the culture as part of learning the ropes. Listening, observing, and asking questions is always a good idea during your first couple of weeks (and beyond since there's always something new to learn—especially if you hope to advance within the company).

What does that have to do with email? Here, too, it's helpful to get a feel for the basic email protocol within your company. The culture of your workplace—formal or casual, or somewhere in between—will usually be reflected in the tone of the emails, so pay attention to how others write. Remember that old expression, "Dress for the job you want, not the job you have"? It's the same principle—communicate like someone who already has the job you aspire to have.

Keep it short and be sensitive to details you include, since it could be shared.

Omit extraneous details and as well as any comments you

wouldn't want others to see. A long-winded email takes up too much of the reader's time and may come across as something they should set aside until they have more time (in which case, they'll probably never read it). If the topic is sensitive or especially complicated, consider suggesting a quick face-to-face meeting, phone call or video chat. "I have a concern about how this client is going to react to the work on this project—do you have a moment to chat about it today so we might be able to discuss a few hurdles?" This way you're less likely to get in trouble for what you wrote but you can be effective with a solution.

Tactical Tip: When you speak via phone, in person or on video chat you can sense nuances that email doesn't allow for. If you must write a long email, be sure to re-read your email two or even three times to make sure you're clear with your words. If the email is very important, it's sometimes also a good idea to have someone proof your email before you send it out.

Write like your email might end up in a PowerPoint.

But Josh, you might be saying, the rules have changed. My colleagues don't even bother with spell check. It's true—the slang and acronyms of texts and Snapchat have infiltrated even the workplace. But I recommend that you resist this trend if you want to be viewed as a professional while also getting your ideas across effectively. Take a few extra seconds to write in complete sentences, spell out words and use proper punctuation when possible. Why? It shows respect to the person or people on the receiving end of your emails, and it's one of the easiest ways I know to look smart and professional.

If your next question is, Sure, I know I need to be professional when communicating with people outside the company—but do I really need to worry about internal emails?, the answer is still "yes." If you regularly send internal emails full of typos, how will your boss know you don't use the same lazy grammar when you communicate with people outside the company, too? So no matter who is the intended recipient might be, treat every email as an opportunity to make a good impression, even if the email is short.

Assume your supervisor sees everything (even if you don't copy them).

It's to everyone's advantage—including yours—to be as transparent as possible with in-office communications. For that matter, assume everyone in the office sees everything. Maybe you've just come out of a long meeting that felt unproductive. By now you should understand why posting your frustration on social media is a bad idea. In this case, sending an email to your best office buddy is also unwise: Wow, could Jerry have possibly dragged out that presentation any longer??

Once you've sent it, you have no control over what happens to that email. You might realize after the fact that you sent it as a group message by mistake. Your friend could forward it to someone else because they think it's funny, or they could leave it up on their desktop, where anybody who passes by (even Jerry) might notice. The worst case scenario is that it's ultimately seen by your boss, who frowns on colleagues making fun at others' expense.

In fact, the reality is that you're misusing office communications at the company's expense. You're causing potential (and completely unnecessary) headaches for your boss, human resources, and other colleagues when you create ill will with another team member. Conversely, when you keep your communications positive and respectful, you'll not only avoid those scenarios, but you'll have a greater chance of being heard when you have a genuine concern about how something's being handled. If you think meetings regularly run too long, it's okay to say so—but in a constructive way that politely shares your concern, the reasoning behind it, and your ideas for making meetings run more smoothly.

Fill out the "to" box in your email last

This is one of my favorite tricks for avoiding email misfires like these:

1. You start to write an email, get distracted and accidentally hit "send" before you're done. If you haven't filled in the "to" box yet, however, this can't happen. So wait until you're finished with the email (and always take a moment to re-read the email two or three times for clarity), and then fill in the recipient.

2. You're addressing a sensitive topic, and it might be wise to wait an hour and re-read when you've had more time to revisit what you really want to say. (This would include any

topic that you're frustrated about, making it doubly important to take a breather in case you want to reconsider the tone after you'd had some time to calm down). Making the "to" box your final step gives you a built-in reminder never to send an email until it's ready.

3. Some emails are just a bad idea. Maybe you had an impulse to complain about a new office policy, or maybe you had an idea for a new project that made perfect sense when it popped into your head—and then 10 minutes later you realized it was impractical, redundant or otherwise a bad idea. These are the types of emails you save in your draft box and someday delete. You got them off your chest—and often that's enough to make you more clear on the issue/subject

---

Tactical Email Tip: Consider writing the email in reverse—start with the body of the email first, then, once you have read it multiple times for clarity, write the subject line and then add in the recipients in the To: and Cc: lines. Not only does this make the email more powerful, but it keeps you from sending the email on accident.

Chapter 8: How to handle negative posts

"Associate with those of good quality if you esteem your own reputation; for it is better to be alone than in bad company."
— George Washington

Here are some key takeaways from this chapter:

- **Think of your search-engine results, especially the first two or three pages, as your "digital curb appeal."** If you have a house to sell, you need it to make a great impression outside in order to draw people in. It's the same with your search results. If you're out doing great volunteer projects and have pictures you could be posting, or you have a great skill to share and could shoot a quick video to post on YouTube to help others, etc., consider using them. Never miss an opportunity to use social media as a way to package yourself online as someone worth getting to know better (or worth taking a second look at for a coveted new spot at a company.)

- **Ask yourself what you want to be known for.** Take the time to sit down and make a list. Then focus on how you can show your priorities, interests, skills and passions on social media. You want some of these to include your professional skills and involvements, but everyone likes to show off their sillier side, too—goofing around with their kids, or playing touch football with friends—and that's great, too. Just keep it Light, Bright, and Polite®, and let your real, authentic self shine and be "discovered" online.

- **Don't fall into the (all-too-common) trap of thinking that avoiding social media is the way to maintain a "clean" reputation.** It won't work. When people can't find you on social media, they miss the opportunity to find out positive things about you—or worse, they wonder if you have something to hide.

- **Build up a personal filter to help decide what should go on social media versus what should be shared with your friends via text or by phone.** Think about the long-term repercussions. Venting online might seem like a good idea in the moment, but stop and ask if you might be offending someone you know without realizing it—such as a friend, or colleague or even your own boss.

Now that you understand the importance of staying on top of your online image, here's something else you need to know: No matter how proactive, thoughtful and strategic you are about your own activities online, other people on social media can undermine it if you're not careful. It's called social media for a reason—Twitter, Facebook, Instagram, blogs, and even consumer review sites are communal spaces. Choices you make on those platforms can make an impact on your reputation. Sometimes things can go wrong when you are engaging with others.

If something goes wrong, you need to have a strategy.

Let's go through a few potential scenarios:

A friend mentions you in a party pic that doesn't help you shine online. There could be any number of reasons a picture doesn't reflect the *you* that you want others—especially employers—to see. Maybe everyone's drinking or the background shows a wild party environment. Maybe your friend added a tagline that was disrespectful to others or offensive in some way. Remember, this is your buddy's post, not yours, so it might be completely unfair for others to judge you by it—but fair or not, there it is. What are you doing to do about it?

Most networks (like Facebook) will alert you through the email address tied to your account or on your activity log when you've been tagged (or mentioned). If you'd rather not have your name associated with the post, the most organic solution is just to contact the person who posted it and ask them to untag you:

Hey, Chris—love the photo you posted last night! Thanks for mentioning me in it. The thing is, a lot of our clients at MediaLeaders are friends or friends-of-friends of mine on Facebook, and I don't like to give them the wrong impression that I'm out partying the night before a big meeting. Also, do you think you could tweak the caption to make more client-friendly? Thanks!

If your friend posted 15 pictures from the event and one of them paints you in a bad light, consider sending this type of email.

> Hey, Steve—Great to see you last week. I noticed you posted photos from the event—would you mind removing this particular one? I'm not sure it shows me in the best possible light or that I'd want clients to see it. Here's a link to the pic I'm referencing: LINK (the link is important—there won't be any question which picture you're talking about, and you're making it easy for your friend to access/delete it). Thanks! See you again soon.

Friends will usually understand and comply—and might be more careful about uploading your picture/tagging you in future posts.

Someone with a similar name (or the same exact name) is giving you a bad reputation.

How? Again, you can control your own online activities, but not others'—even if they happen to have the same name.

Here's an example. I speak to a lot of teens and parents each year about these very issues, in their case because college admissions officers—like employers and potential employers—will look at their online reputation. The most common question I hear from these students?

I'm not on social media, so I'm fine, right? People will only judge me/my application based on what I actually submit

because I don't share anything online.

Here is the quickest way to see the error in this thinking, and it's advice I give all the time:

Search for yourself online and see what shows up on the first 3 pages of Google. The answer—and I am 100 percent positive of this—is not going to be "nothing."

Instead, they'll probably find information, pictures, posts and other online activity by somebody with the same or a similar name. It's inevitable, because the Internet is a big and crowded place. If you happen to have "name twins" who might be posting hateful speech, inappropriate photos, or anything else you don't want to be associated with, while you lack any social media presence at all, their posts are the ones that will show up when people search for you. And you can't assume that people will know the difference. If someone you don't even know can hurt your reputation just by having a similar name, then obviously your attempt to stay "clean" on social media has failed.

When I talk to young people who are applying for college, grad school or their first job, this can be a big problem, because the admissions officers or potential employers who are actively searching for prospects on the Internet could easily get confused about whether or not the person they're finding is really you. And, this is exactly the feedback I get from college admissions officers (and employers).

If you're a professional, however, you might be tempted to think this doesn't apply to you. Josh, c'mon. My supervisor knows me—he or she is not going to confuse me with someone else they find on the Internet, even if they do have a similar name.

That might be true, but do you really want to risk your reputation on the assumption that they'll always know which Jane Doe is you and which is not? **Imagine there's someone with your name who lives in the same area and might even share vaguely similar physical characteristics—again, the Internet is a large and crowded space—and this person is regularly posting offensive opinions, tacky pictures or anything else you may not want to be associated with.** Maybe your supervisor sees this. He or she is not very likely to come out and ask you—Hey Jane, is this you who posted this? And if they suspect it is you, it could ultimately hurt your chances for future advances.

And that's just your supervisor. Your clients or people higher up in the company might not know you well at all—maybe they've never even seen you in person. They could easily confuse you with your name twins.

The end result is that while you're busy trying to protect yourself by staying away from social media, others are building a digital reputation for you...and it might not be the reputation you want.

You've put at least some effort into posting positive things on social media, but no one notices because they're hidden behind less-positive results.

Here's a real estate analogy. Shows like "Flip this House" are hugely popular because real estate has become a national pastime. People especially love the idea of taking a home that needs a lot of love and turning it into a knockout property. So try to imagine that your online reputation is like a house you want to sell. It's a charming house with a lot of great features—but the yard hasn't been maintained to its full potential, and the trim is in need of a paint job.

But you're a busy professional, and worrying about the home's exterior seems like a hassle. Besides, the inside looks pretty good—and that's what counts, right?

The reality is that the exterior of your home (just like the first two pages of your search results) is incredibly important. If the outside looks neglected, it will make a negative first impression, so, don't be surprised if the response from potential buyers is slow or nonexistent. Most Realtors will tell you that curb appeal is what gets people in the door so they can discover all the wonderful qualities inside. And often you can improve the curb appeal with just a little effort. Things like adding relatively inexpensive landscaping, a fresh coat of paint on the shutters or a new flag hung outside can make a big difference.

Your online reputation works much the same way. **No matter how many great skills and personal qualities you have, these days many people's first impression of you will come from your online reputation**—and if they don't like what they see at first glance, they (especially employers) might move onto the next prospect for a job or promotion opportunity.

You should take the time to step out onto the street and look at your "digital home" from the perspective of someone searching for you. You may realize you want to manage and improve it, not ignore it and hope no one notices the weeds. When it comes to the Internet, your "digital curb appeal" comes from the listings on the first two or three pages of your search-engine results, combined with any other social media activity your boss might be privy to. Just as a home's exterior can make the difference between prospective buyers scheduling a viewing or skipping ahead to the next listing, your online reputation can either create or kill opportunities. Would you really want to leave it up to chance when so much is at stake?

Three smart and strategic steps for creating the image you want

1. **Know how others view you online.** If you want to sell a home, you need to know how potential buyers see it from the street. So when you think about your online reputation, getting an objective view of your own search results is step one for absolutely everybody.

   If I ask an auditorium full of people how many have searched for themselves online, most will raise their hands. But they might not be getting the same results that others see. For one, search engines like Google follow your own online activity on personal computers or devices, so they tend to skew your results towards things they know interest you based on your most common searches. For another, you might not be searching for the same exact version of your name and/or keywords that other people might search.

When I was running for politics in 2009 I knew people would search for me online after they met me on their doorstep. I set out to have the very best Google results I could find and came up with a few techniques to do so. I thought to myself, "Wouldn't it be nice if I had something like an online reputation assistant to email me every week and remind me to search for myself online—and then make it fast and easy by providing links that take me directly to Google and perform the search with the push of a button?"

So I built a small tool for myself that works just like that—I receive the weekly emails and can see my footprint without having to enter redundant information in the search box over and over. It worked great to help me shine online. I quickly found some results I didn't want online and was able to address them either by removing them outright or using another effective technique, which is flooding the Internet with positive results that pushed what I didn't like back to pages four, five or even deeper into the Google Sphere.

Eventually, I renamed the tool and opened it up for friends and clients. Now, you can sign up to search for yourself at FootprintFridayTool.com, which I mentioned earlier. You simply fill in the relevant information about yourself, and we'll send you an email every Friday with buttons you can click to obtain a complete picture of your online footprint. Footprint Friday enables you to fill in some simple information about yourself, including variations of your name and keywords such as your alma mater or profession, and we'll send you an email reminder every Friday along with buttons you can push that will bring up your real-time search results.

2. **Create a plan.** The online results you find for yourself today are like the curb appeal of your house. It might be ugly and neglected. It might be okay but still feel like it's missing something, like a spec house where the builder chose not to invest in landscaping. Or maybe it's somewhere in between, but chances are, there's room for improvement.

   The goal, of course, is to make it look great—but also look like you. You want it to reflect your tastes and interests (and be authentic).

   Again, you can use the same strategy with your online reputation. You start with what you have and make it better. Begin by outlining your goals. How do you want to be seen by others who search for you online?

   So get ready to make a plan.

3. **Make a list of 5 professional and personal activities/traits that would look great to your employer.** What do you want to be discovered doing?

What do you want your online brand to look like?

I want to be known as a PR professional.

What is a PR professional known for?

- Having a LinkedIn profile that is up-to-date and professional.

- Tweeting from time to time about PR tips and trends— sharing great information while establishing your credibility in the field.

- Joining professional organizations. (Do your own research on organizations that are out there, but it never hurts also to ask your supervisor for his or her suggestions about the ones they recommend and like to see company representatives associated with.)

- Participating in conferences in your field (again, with your supervisor's permission), volunteering to participate in panel discussions or agreeing to be interviewed for a blog or article about your area of expertise.

These are activities that tend to be shared on social media, through the organization's own websites/posts and elsewhere, so they tend to rank high in search results thanks to their social media sharing activities.

I want to be known for giving back by using my professional skills.

It's great when you can use skills from your career to help others—in the case of a PR professional, this might be helping a nonprofit get the word out about fundraising events, improving their website or helping with a social media campaign. It's a win-win, allowing you to use your skills in a new context (which is always a great learning experience) and help organizations in the community that are important to you but often lack a PR budget. In the process, while getting a great chance to help with something you care about you will be noticed doing good on social media.

I want to be known for giving back to the community.

It's great to let people know about other causes you're passionate about outside your career, too. If you're involved in groups that are helping others, these are other great opportunities to take photos. Just make sure the causes you associate yourself with online are not controversial. If you're volunteering for a major political party and actively advertise it on social media, you could risk alienating half the people who see your posts. But if you're involved with the local Boys & Girls Club, Habitat for Humanity or volunteering at a local soup kitchen, go ahead and post about your passion. Just be sure to thank the organization and other volunteers for the opportunity. You want to make the post about them, not you, which could come across as self-serving (and unnecessary since it's already posted under your name and picture). Another tip to make the social media posts more humble is to tell the story of the outcome, and not about how you served. Instead of saying "I had a great day feeding the homeless today!" consider saying, "Thank you to the L.A. Chapter of the XYZ org for letting my friends and me serve today. With everyone's generous help, we were able to serve 100 people in need." The story of the outcome is something that resonates better online (especially when you are a very small part of it and you're cheerleading everyone else involved).

I have a family and I want to share photos on social media so my distant relatives can stay updated on our family activities (and how quickly my kids are growing up).

I don't mind if my boss sees this because I don't mind being known as family oriented. There's a good chance your boss likes to see you're family oriented and enjoy a healthy work/life balance. Photos of your children are terrific in moderation (and remember that the best ones highlight interesting things you might do together as a family, such as whitewater rafting or traveling to unusual locations). Be sure to think before you post, "does this photo share too much info about my child's birth date or where we live?" If not, and you feel comfortable with others seeing it, then go ahead and share a family photo once a week.

I want to be known for having interesting skills or hobbies.

For me, others are sometimes surprised to learn that I enjoy (and have learned to be fairly good at) fixing broken appliances. It's unrelated to my profession, but I like the puzzle-solving aspect of it, the chance to learn new skills and the ability to teach others. My older Jeep Grand Cherokee had frosted headlights. I took it to the dealership and learned it costs about $350 for new headlamps. I did some research online and found I could buy the headlamps myself on Amazon for about $80 (with free shipping, no less). I took the leap, ordered the headlamps and recorded all of the steps I took to upgrade my car. Why? Because while searching for the headlamps, I'd noted that several other people had questions about the same process, and I knew a video would be a fun way to share what I'd learned. I edited the footage down to a four-minute video and taught others how I fixed my car while saving $250+. Now my little video has received over 15,500 views on YouTube. Although this skill isn't directly tied to my career, if my clients saw the video, they would like that I'm helping others with my skills (and they might be impressed that it got so much traction).

You might think that in this "what I want to be known for"

example for a PR professional, three of the five items listed are unrelated to professional advancement. But in reality, it all ties together. We've already talked about how posting wild party pics all over social media could make an employer think twice before giving you more professional responsibility. By contrast, activities that showcase your giving, creative side online can create the kind of reputation companies want to see in their employees—even when it's seemingly unrelated to their job duties. (Case in point: How many professional bios do you see on company websites that mention an employee's outside service work, volunteer positions and family life? Company PR people like to show their team members as skilled and competent at what they do—but also having skills and passions related to their community, family life, etc.)

To emphasize the point, a friend of mine recently listed me as a reference when he was applying for a new job. Paul is in tech sales, so when the prospective employer called me, I gave him a glowing reference for his skills and past performance in that area. But before we hung up, I also shared an additional trait of Paul's that I feel speaks volumes about his dedication and character: He has coached almost every one of his young son's baseball and soccer teams over the last 5 years. He volunteers countless hours of his time on practice nights during the week and coaches games on weekends, and he's known as the guy every parent wants their kid to play for because of his positive mentorship skills (not to mention, his son has turned out to be a wonderful athlete who sets a good example for other kids).

At the end of the call, the employer I was talking with said they very much appreciated that personal story since it was authentic. It also probably gave the employer something fun to talk about with Paul in further discussions.

As a business owner myself, I'm very interested in knowing that my employees have positive outside interests and are well-rounded people who will bring interesting perspectives to the team. That's why I encourage people to sit down and think about what they really want to be known for online and to make it a mix of professional and positive personal stories. It's the best way to put your best, authentic self forward online and stay focused on the positive and grateful aspects of what you do every day. It's also another way to own your search results. **The more times your name shows up in a positive way, the further down you push any negative results.** Negative results include things we've discussed earlier in this chapter such as posts your friends have tagged you in without your consent; posts you made yourself and later came to regret (but still exist because they were shared); or posts from your "name twins"...those people with a name like yours who could be confused with you.

So how do you avoid adding new posts that you won't be proud of later—the ones that undermine the positive posts you've been working so hard to add and push to the top of your search pages? One of my goals is to help you build up a personal filter that helps you decide what should go on social media, and what should be shared with your friends via text or phone call instead.

Here's an example of a personal filter issue you may have seen on social media:

1. Have you ever had a friend who got frustrated and wanted to share their frustration online? For instance, perhaps they shared on Facebook: "Employees at Clothing Store X are so lazy. Tried to shop there today, and no one lifted a finger to help me. How do these people even have jobs?"

2. Take a moment to think how that appeared online. It's perfectly natural for us to want to vent when we have a bad customer-service experience. Sometimes sharing our frustrations online is the easiest way to express our frustration. But then imagine what might have happened to our friend a few hours after she posted her angry rant:

3. A few of their friends started piling on. "So true. I never shop there," her BFF wrote. "Their clothes aren't cool anymore, anyway. People should be embarrassed to work there."

4. Then imagine your friend woke up the next day, checked her feed and noticed this: "You know, my mom/sister/friend works there. Maybe you should consider that it's a stressful job and they're understaffed during this season." Most likely, your friend had no idea they knew anyone who worked at that store (nor did they think someone would see this and publicly shame them over their comment.)

5. Your friend then realized Clothing Store X actually does business with her employer—and somebody at Clothing Store X let her employer know they don't appreciate this kind of social media bad mouthing from a company they work with.

Obviously, your friend wouldn't be thinking about any of this when she first posted her rant. But if she had thought about the potential fallout ahead of time, she'd be more likely to consider she had other options, such as calling/texting a friend to complain or even calling the store manager personally and having a constructive conversation. In many cases (and I encourage this at our company), an employer appreciates the chance to directly listen and apologize for a bad experience from a customer rather than to see it hashed out on social media. Also, some employers might even be so thankful for the tip/complaint that they will offer a discount or something to make it right, and you'll save face by not coming across as someone who carelessly criticizes businesses without giving them even a chance to hear you out privately.

In other words, thinking through the longer-term consequences of your online actions is another helpful technique for building your filter and saving yourself and others grief down the road. And when you do this, here's another interesting thing you might notice: Whatever satisfaction you feel from venting your anger toward another person or organization is usually fleeting. But if you don't post it, often you can look back the next day and feel good for having taken the high road.

As I've said before, you are a human being with real feelings. But you may avoid problems online if you consider deciding where to post a rant versus a positive feeling.

We all have a bad day sometimes, and you really should have the chance to tell someone (and hopefully get feedback from someone that cares). It is okay to vent privately.

Please note, I don't want you to be fake online. Instead, I just want you to know when something should be posted online (instead of texted).

Remember earlier when I mentioned the technique I call "Is it a text or a tweet?"

You may have a terrible experience with a person or a business and want to tell someone. Instead of complaining on Twitter/Facebook or somewhere public, consider calling or texting or sitting down to coffee with someone. Then, vent away! Tell them how frustrated you are about the situation. Since they are a close friend, they will hopefully listen and not judge. Once you have shared your feelings with them, you're probably going to feel a lot better. The next day you will also be better equipped to deal with the situation while not hurting your online reputation (or the reputation of the other party).

Are you monitoring your online image?

Register for our FREE Footprint Friday tool to manage your online brand each week in less than 5 minutes.

Visit FootprintFridayTool.com

Chapter 9: How to set a good example for kids

"The greatest reward for your actions is not the respect you gain from others but the respect you gain for yourself." — T-Jay Taylor

---

This is a set of excerpts from my previous book that helps parents to safely navigate social media with their Teens: Light, Bright & Polite #2: How to Use Social Media to Impress Colleges & Future Employers

I mentioned before that I spend a lot of my time speaking to schools and groups around the country that invite me to share my message with students and parents so they can be safe and smart on social media. People are so hungry for this information—because they recognize the tremendous difference it can make in the life of a tween or teen—that I've also written a previous book for parents on the subject: Light, Bright & Polite: How to Use Social Media to Impress Colleges & Future Employers.

And just as I learned when I was running for city council in Hermosa Beach, I've seen again and again that these are not just strategies for students. In fact, parents often come up after they hear my presentation about teenagers and social media to tell me they've learned things they (or their neighbors, family members, and colleagues) can use in their own lives. The reality is there are many adults who don't fully understand how easily information travels on the Internet, how it can harm them and how others perceive the information.

Learning to be social media savvy as a family

My hope is that in following the advice in this book, you will not only benefit yourself but pass it on to others, especially your kids or students. And the best way to do that is to be a good social media role model yourself. (Speaking of which, when I address large groups of students, I often ask them, "How many of you have searched online for your own parents?" More than 40% of them have. Are you comfortable with what they'll find? Do you set a good example for how you want them to conduct themselves online, knowing what's at stake for their future?)

I recommend reading Light, Bright & Polite: How to Use Social Media to Impress Colleges & Future Employers along with your teen to gain additional tips, so you can both learn how to become better managers of your own online brands. You can get a copy of it at JoshOchs.com. Our family version of Footprint Friday is something that might help you monitor your kids online. The free tool can be found at FootprintFriday.com. Each week you can compare notes to see if you're pleased with the week's results, or if needed, brainstorm ways to fix any problem areas that might have cropped up. Think of creating great online search results as a goal you can work on together.

How to talk to your kids about social media

As I've mentioned, there's a myth that avoiding social media somehow creates a pristine digital footprint. But that's not how it works. In Chapter 1 we talked about the fact that people who look for you online and find nothing rarely think, "Oh, this person must be so busy doing great things in the community, they don't have time for social media." Instead, they're more likely to think you're disengaged from your community—or even have a reason to try and stay out of public view.

Parents are often the most common culprits in trying to enforce this idea of complete Internet privacy for their kids, which is understandable—especially if they've only heard horror stories about kids "talking" with or even meeting sketchy people they meet online, or getting in trouble as a result of something they posted.

Keeping your kids off of social media altogether—or worse, trying to keep them in the dark about it—could ultimately cause more harm than good. Let me explain.

Chances are, even if you ban social media from your home (and avoid having a healthy dialog about it), your kids are still exposed to it elsewhere. So they can end up opening their own accounts without you knowing it (or talking with them about it beforehand). In that case, you might have done exactly what you meant to avoid, which is to send them out into cybersphere to create a digital footprint without any guidance. Instead, once you do open a dialog (which begins with educating yourself), you can show your tweens and teens there are positive ways to use the Internet to call attention to good causes, show gratitude to others, demonstrate skills they have (potentially to college admissions officers), and shine online in a way that's authentic.

But Josh, how do I start a dialog?

If your kids are old enough to start posting things publicly online (which is a personal decision to be made as a family, but age 14 is a good general rule of thumb for many kids), start having regular discussions with them about their social media accounts in general—and don't forget to put an emphasis on working with them and not against them. Let them teach you all about the social media platforms they use so that they can feel like they are the expert at something. Ask them who some of their followers are, and how they decide what to post and why. Inevitably, there will be something that they have posted—or something that one of their friends have posted with them in the picture—that will make them uncomfortable for you to see. Anything they cringe at showing you probably shouldn't be on their account in the first place but can be a great place to continue a conversation about how they can shine online.

Parents can start a conversation that shows their kids how being LBP can make them more popular through a clean online reputation. Sometimes it's hard to connect with our kids or know how to say things in a way that they will understand, but it's very important for us to make it understandable on their level. When working with kids, consider avoiding the use of these buzz terms that were created by Fortune 500 marketing departments: "digital citizen" and "digital literacy." These words aren't a part of the usual middle school or high school level conversation, and they are not going to resonate with teenagers based on their current experiences.

What are some ways to keep the dialog open?

1. **Give kids some space on social media.** They might not tell you this, but your kids probably value social media as a way to communicate with their friends (not mom and dad). So if you see that your daughter posts something on social media, don't rush in with a comment: "Hi honey, love you, see you tonight!" That's why you see kids going to other apps to find their own space.

2. **Instead, be a little passive. Just "listen" on social media—almost like a secret spy.** This is one of the few times I would advocate that, but in this case, it's okay. The more you bring up or respond to every little thing you see, the more they're going to try and hide it from you. Wouldn't you rather keep this direct connection you have to your kids a bit in reserve, and use it as a secret power that you have in case something goes wrong?

If I feel like I just don't know enough about certain social media apps to even start a discussion, how else can I learn?

First, you can just research the app you want to talk to your kid about using Google. **Search for the app name and click on the "news" tab at the top of the search result to see what journalists say about the app.** Click on the "video" button at the top of the Google search to learn how the app works. There is so much information online that you can find in less than 10 minutes.

Second, you can visit SafeSmartSocial.com, and watch free videos to learn about the most popular apps your kids might be exposed to.

Third, get your kids involved by asking them to teach you how an app works. Once you've got the basic idea of what the app does, you can "play dumb" and ask your kids to explain it to you in more detail. Kids love feeling like the expert and you will learn about the app in their terms, which will help you relate to them even more.

> **Tactical Tip when talking with Teens:** When learning something new from a kid, try not to say, "Why would I ever want to do that?" Instead, say, "Cool, what happens when I do that?" When parents are learning and they ask "why," it tends to make them sound out of touch and puts up a communication barrier. This may make your kid less likely to approach you if something goes wrong, because they don't think you get why someone would use the app anyway. How could you possibly understand now that there's a problem?

If you see your kids posting on a new app, ask them to walk you through their online profile and their most recent seven posts. Ask them about some of the photos and have them explain how they think others would perceive them. Let them take the driver's seat in this exercise so they feel comfortable. When they describe the photo, it makes them take ownership of the images, and they sometimes will self-correct and see what you see (without you having to seem negative). All you have to do is have them teach you how the app works and what they are posting. Usually, they will come to their own conclusions if you guide the conversation.

Twenty years ago kids didn't want you to read their diary. Today, many students post their innermost secrets on their social media accounts and are okay with diary-like content being seen by all of their friends. Tweens and teens have become accustomed to seeing their friends share their selfies and embarrassing personal details for everyone to see. Their friends get some sort of thrill out of sharing their innermost secrets online to elicit a response. In many cases, kids are better at engaging their followers than Fortune 500 brands that I've been speaking to over the last decade, since the brands are very cautious and corporate online. Kids, on the other hand, are good at sharing their online "diary" because they like the instant feedback it gives them. These apps reward those that share interesting personal information.

Nowadays there isn't any sneaking around to find (and read) a student's diary. Instead, kids sometimes post their most private moments on their social media accounts for everyone to see (or for a college to eventually find). All a parent needs to do is "friend" their kid online, become an observer and read their kids' posts. So, to keep your "diary reading privileges" intact, consider not commenting directly on your kids' posts. Instead, use those posts to start a dialog around those issues and topics with your kids in real life (maybe around the dinner table or on the car ride home).

Find someone you trust to talk with your kids.

If you are having a hard time connecting with your kid on this topic, consider that you might not be the best fit for the job right now. It may be that there's another parent (whom you trust) who can talk to your kids about being safe and putting their best foot forward. Or, you can use one of your adult friends, someone your kid knows and you trust, and this person can have a meaningful conversation with them about social media. Also, consider other people in your family who might have more knowledge on the topic. You could use a "cool" favorite aunt or uncle. I hope to someday be this "cool" uncle to my nieces and nephews.

Whoever is talking to your kids, start by setting some goals. Have an important talk about which colleges and/or careers most excite them, for example. By talking about long-term goals, you will help them start to understand their long-term picture. Your chosen mentor can ask your kids what types of online posts and photos might impress those colleges and/or employers. In general, you and/or your appointed stand-in can take this opportunity to talk to your kids about keeping their online image positive and full of gratitude to impress these groups in the future—a great way to motivate your kids to care.

10 takeaways from my Teen/Parent book

Light, Bright & Polite: How to Use Social Media to Impress Colleges & Future Employers to help set goals for your kids and your whole family

For example, here are a few of the tips included in my

previous book for parents of teens and professionals that they can work on together:

1. **How to motivate your kids (and stay motivated yourself) to care about your social media posts:** To start, pick a long-term goal that your kid has. You could start a conversation like this: "You love football. Would you like to play football in college? Where do you want to go to college? Do you think that college (and the coach) will search for you online? What kind of posts do you think the coach might like to see?" This puts their social media usage into an entirely new perspective. Now, instead of just thinking about whether you or their friends like their posts, your kids are thinking long term about how other people like teachers, coaches, and employers will view their posts.

2. **There's no such thing as an expiration date on social media.** If you post something on Facebook and later think better of it, you can delete it, right? Or what about Snapchat, which promises to destroy your post, Mission-Impossible style, after it's been seen? These features lull users into a false sense of security with their built-in content expiration features—but people can, in one second, take a screenshot of a post before it expires or is removed and post it somewhere else to exist forever on your Google results. Consider bloggers who might have a bone to pick with you: Anything posted online that offends certain communities is sure to be blogged about right away (with the content archived indefinitely).

3. **Establish a consistent image across all your profiles— beginning with your picture.** When colleges search for you, they want to quickly be assured they found the right account. They are searching for hundreds of applicants

each day, and when you have different selfies for each network you're going to make it difficult for them to find the real you. Seeing the same photo on each account makes it easier for colleges to connect the dots between all of your professional, fun, relevant forms of social media. Make sure that your photo is clear, well lit, and highlights only you (obscure group photos will not help you.) When in doubt, ask a mentor or friend for their thoughts on the best photo.

4. **Avoid political topics.** Make sure that your kid considers the risk of sharing any political viewpoints anywhere public on social media—and that you consider the risk of doing this yourself. (Here's a hint: the risks are very, very high. In a politically divided country where you can never assume you know another person's political views and how they might differ from yours, people can and do lose friends and school or job opportunities, often without knowing why, because of a political rant they posted online.)

But if you talk politics on your Facebook page, your kids are going to feel more comfortable sharing their own controversial opinions with their online friends. It doesn't matter what side you're on; you have almost a 50/50 chance of being on the opposite camp of the person you or your child is trying to impress. Most people fail to think about this when they post on social media. At the same time, when discussing politics, most people also become super passionate and even defensive in their viewpoint. Naturally, no one wants to feel their worldview is wrong. Since political rants can reflect some of our most deeply held opinions, they are not always expressed in a rational manner—in fact, they can come across as very negative. Do you think your friends or future employer will comment on your posts, looking for more information about why you feel so strongly, trying to see your point of view? No. They will simply take a mental note that you are willing to share controversial opinions on your social media accounts for all to see (and many times those opinions are somewhat close-minded.) For every person who agrees with you on politics, chances are there are at least two who are offended and taking note of your stance. Sometimes, even people on your same side of the issue can notice how dramatic you are in your argument and avoid commenting because it may drag them down and make them look careless in their own online brand.

Tactical Tip: You should vent, but instead of using Twitter/Facebook, consider venting about political opinions to your close friends via text message or in person.

---

5. **Own your image by volunteering your camera to take group photos.** When I ran for politics I would always want to post the best photo of the group while also managing my reputation. Since I always had a camera or cell phone with me, before a group photo, I'd be the one to volunteer, "Use my phone." This lets me always be in the photo, but also lets me control what kind of pictures were posted (since they all lived on my phone/camera). That way, no crazy or inappropriate pictures started to circulate online or otherwise. I became my own brand manager and helped my friends stand out online in a positive way, too.

6. **Wait until after events to post your photos.** If you attend a lot of fun events, you may have a lot of photos to post. Consider waiting until the next day (or the end of your event) to post any of your event photos. This gives you

---

time to think of a great description, and you get to pick the best photo that you took. You could even use your favorite app to clear up the photo. This also helps you to be less distracted while you're at the event so that you don't miss possibly another great opportunity to take an additional photo. Lastly, you'll have a chance the next day to be a good friend on social media and select the photo where all of your friends also shine online. This helps you stand out since you're managing your own brand (and that of your friends) online.

7. **YouTube is a great platform when you use it well— especially since it is owned by Google and is given an unfair advantage in search results.** Share videos of volunteer events or videos that add value for those who might watch it, for instance. But as a professional, avoid posting funny videos you made to entertain your friends or drudged up to relive the glory days of college. Be sure to include your name in the video title if you want it to come up in search results on Google. Also be sure to look over your YouTube account to make sure it doesn't show a trail of "liking" inappropriate videos.

8. **Always weed out those old posts!** There is no harm in deleting stale content when it doesn't fairly represent who you are today, especially when it can help you shine online to a potential employer.

9. Jim Ellis, Dean of the USC Marshall School of Business suggests: **Don't permanentize any angry/hurtful sentiments.** Every time you put things in writing you permanentize your actions. Anything that goes on the web stays out there for someone to find. It's better to take five minutes to calm down and reconsider whether you should unleash your hurt feelings on someone else

because when you complain online or post in a dramatic way, you walk around with a black cloud over your head on social media that others can follow.

Instead, be thoughtful in the messages you post/send. For example, be a positive leader in something. Use social media to your advantage to build your name/image online. Being a thought leader means taking something that you are already good at and sharing it with other people so that you can help them to be good at it, too.

10. **Ask yourself, "Would I be comfortable with my future college seeing all of my online friends?"** The best online friends are those who you feel totally comfortable having over for dinner to meet your family and/or parents (or being on your college application). If you don't know if your parents or family would approve of them, then be careful before accepting them as your "friend" online since they can see all of your information. Meanwhile, as the saying goes, people (or colleges) may judge you by the company you keep (and the posts you share)—even if they're only social media contacts. It only makes sense to carefully select who you are publicly associated with on your public accounts.

Those are just 10 examples, but the point is that **while students might use different apps than you do, post about different topics, or sometimes even seem to speak a different language than you do, search engines treat everyone the same.** So whatever your immediate goal is—whether it's getting into your one of your first-choice schools or landing a coveted promotion—my goal is always to try and share the timeless advice I've learned over years of personal experience about how you can use social media to your advantage in an authentic manner.

The key message is very simple. You're never too young or too old to gain a competitive advantage by using social media to present your best, authentic self to shine online.

Are you monitoring your online image?

Register for our FREE Footprint Friday tool to manage your online brand each week in less than 5 minutes.

Visit FootprintFridayTool.com

GET FREE ACCESS TO OUR ONLINE BRANDING TOOL

READ THIS

Just to say thanks for buying this book, I would like to give you free access to my online tool that helps you monitor your online image.

TO ACCESS OUR FREE TOOL GO TO:
FootprintFridayTool.com

This tool will show you all the online results other people will discover about you.

Thank you to the following people that helped to make this book possible:

Elisa Croft: Your content marketing skills, event production skills and website skills are incredible. I am so fortunate to have you on our team and I adore your positive attitude. Helping me to manage everything has given me time to write this book. Thanks!

Aoife Teague: Thank you for helping us to coordinate our 2017 conferences and for proofing much of our content.

Linda-Marie Koerner: Thank you for helping us to coordinate content and proofread. You're a great writer and have valuable ideas.

Notes

Notes

Tag @JoshOchs on social

Notes

Tag @JoshOchs on social

Notes

Tag @JoshOchs on social

Notes

Tag @JoshOchs on social

Notes

Notes

Tag @JoshOchs on social

Notes

Tag @JoshOchs on social

Notes

Tag @JoshOchs on social

Notes

Tag @JoshOchs on social

Notes

Notes

Tag @JoshOchs on social

Notes

Tag @JoshOchs on social

Notes

Tag @JoshOchs on social

Made in the USA
San Bernardino, CA
23 March 2017